Marion -
Snap Conference
2013
Julie Swope

Of Roots and Wings

Julie D. Swope

ISBN: 1475154658
ISBN-13: 9781475154658

Library of Congress Control Number: 2012906378
CreateSpace, North Charleston, SC

For my mother, Kathleen O'Melia - she didn't give me roots, but gave me wings.

This book is a collection of memoirs. But beyond *Of Roots and Wings* is a powerful study of psychological relationships across a lifetime.

I finished *Of Roots and Wings* in 2009 but have left it unpublished until now. It's not easy to share one's life and bare one's soul; however with the support and encouragement of many friends and family, I chose to pass the gifts of hope, perseverance, and tenacity to others.

Much gratitude to my four parents, brothers, sisters, and especially my children, all of whom have wings of their own.

Much gratitude to my friends Nancy Altland, Diana Beasley, Ross, Libbie and Dina Falzone, Earl Atlas Glover, Jesse and Joyce Grimm, Dan Ingram, Pat and Shelly Kaplan, Patricia B. Learned, Jean Rutledge and Jack Van Newkirk for their consistent support. Also to Judy Wolfman, who helped clean up my original manuscript of my Pennsylvania dutchiness.

Special thanks to Joan Maruskin, who continues to be an inspiration every day of my life. I have always been propelled by encouragement, so lastly - thanks to everyone throughout my lifetime who said, "Julie, you should write a book."

Fond memories of Sue Bernstein, J. Christian Ness, Tom Rosenberg, and Aisha Sharif, all of whom had a major impact on my life and were called to another life much too soon.

Hmmm - is there more to tell between 2009 and now ? Who's to say.

Some names have been changed to protect the innocent; some names have been changed to protect the guilty from causing further damage to the innocent. Any similarities to anyone guilty, either living or dead, are merely coincidental.

CONTENTS

CHAPTER 1: THE ORPHANAGE

My father was an alcoholic, and my mother was mentally and emotionally unable to care for and protect her children. My siblings and I became named defendants before the Juvenile Court of Schuylkill County in Pennsylvania, in a prosecution for neglected dependency brought by Elmer Kaiser, the Supervising Principal for the Porter Township School District; Israel Yost, a pastor; and Leroy Kopp, a local police officer. The Juvenile Court's order was signed by Judge Dalton, December 20, 1949, who ordered us (Connie, Thomas, Alvin, Allan, Ivan, Nancy, Beverly, and Georgina Stauffer) to be committed to the St. Francis Orphan Asylum and detained there until further order of the court.

I, Beverly, was twenty- three months old. Seventeen years later I learned from my oldest sister, Connie, that four brothers and two sisters arrived there with me. Connie, at age ten, was the oldest sibling. Upon our arrival at St. Francis, Sister Spaciosa, the mother superior, greeted us. She lined us up, anointed each of us with holy water, and gave us the evil eye as if we seven children were of little account. Perhaps we were deficient in her evil eyes since the orphanage was Catholic and we were Protestant. Mother S.'s hands were folded in prayer as she looked to the heavens, heaved a big sigh, and called us heathens. From that day forward, she made examples of us to the other children: we were beaten, locked in closets, made to take cold showers, and given heavy chores. We raged silently inside; the rule was that children were never permitted to display their anger.

St. Francis was divided into sections: the section for pre-schoolers, which covered ages two to five, and the school-age section, which housed children six to fourteen. Boys and girls were segregated. Since my brothers and sisters were of various ages, we didn't see each other regularly. Large white pillars on the oak floors of the big common bedrooms served as natural partitions.

"Sometimes the pillars come to life," explained Sister Bartholomew (whom we later called Sister B.) with a twinkle in her eye.

"Come to life?" I asked, "What do you mean?"

"Well, if you have a good day, they are angels guarding you. But if you have a bad day, the bad spirits are there to punish you." I always saw them as angels, though Sister B. disputed my perception.

At bedtime, under the watchful eye of Mother S., the older children tucked in the younger ones. Our hands had to remain on top of the bedspread, arms at our sides and palms down, throughout the night. One girl didn't understand.

"Why do we have to have our hands outside the covers?" she asked.

"So you can't put your hands in your pajama bottoms," Mother S. said. "It's a sin to touch yourself."

I was twenty- three months old and in the little girl's section. I was rambunctious and frequently climbed out of my white iron crib; so they moved me into a kid's bed. I was permitted to be in Mother S.'s office and to eat with her and the other nuns. I saw her thrash other children using her long rosary beads and the white cords she wore around her waist. Her wrath didn't bother me. Since I was Mother S.'s favorite, she was fond of taking me to her bed at night. She carried me in her arms down the long corridors then shut the door and put me down gently on her bed. She undressed me and secured my covers under the mattress. She wasn't mean; she was nice. Her finger touched her lips.

“Shhh, remember to be quiet,” she whispered. “Now turn and face the wall while I get undressed.”The rule was to be silent. She climbed into bed and snuggled up against me. I didn't feel cloth, cords, or rosary beads. Mother S. laid me on top of her; she placed a nipple in my mouth and told me to suck her. I was quiet, but she wasn't. She moaned softly and sounded like a purring cat. I was happy that she was nice to me. Then she shifted me to her other breast and repeated the soft sounds. On some nights she would push my head gently down her body until my toes touched hers.

“Touch me between my legs. Lick me,” she whispered. She continuously moaned softly. During that time I fantasized that she was my mother and I wasn't in the orphanage. I was happy; I knew I was not a *heathen*—I had worth. I became familiar with her room and wondered why she could be nice only in her bedroom.

“Face the wall,” she whispered when she tired of me. She got up from the bed, and I could I hear the sound of water coming from the spigots. She returned with her nightshirt on and wiped my hands and face with a washcloth. She then put my pajamas on me and buttoned them from top to bottom. The dream would end for the night until the next time. She carried me back to my bed, where she tucked me in tightly and placed my arms and hands outside the covers, just like all the other children. I knew, however, that I wasn't like the others, for my arms and hands had touched her. I was special; the other girls had to sleep while I stayed awake.

Georgina, my younger sister, arrived at the orphanage on August 14, 1950. She had been placed previously at Saint Joseph's Children's Hospital in Scranton, Pennsylvania, and now joined us. I was vocal, and Georgina was silent. I was active; she was inactive. I didn't like to sleep; she slept through the night and took two naps during the day. Georgina pulled her right earlobe and bit her lower lip to soothe herself, stopping only to eat meals, use the bathroom, or sleep.

Some nights I awoke in the middle of the night and noticed Georgina wasn't in her bed or on the window ledge. I realized Georgina had taken my place in Mother S.'s bed. I left my bed at night hoping for Mother S. to return, but the door was locked. I climbed onto the window ledge and looked at the moon, stars, and clouds. I wanted to be with them. I fell asleep and was awakened the next morning by a nun yanking my arm or pulling my hair. I began to masturbate and soil myself; once again I had the attention of Mother S..

"What are you doing?" she shouted, pulling my arm. "We don't do that! It's nasty and dirty. Stop it this moment! You must be possessed by Satan," she shrieked, wagging her finger at me. I had no idea what she meant by that. That was when I learned my first color, red, and I learned it in an unusual way. Mother S. made me wear red socks while other kids wore white ones. The red identified me as a creature from the devil, and the children were instructed to ignore me. Once when I fell in the stairwell, another girl helped me up. She was beaten for befriending me. Thus I learned that Mother superior proved to be inferior.

I built a glass wall to separate myself from the others and watched them play while I sat alone on the playground. But I told myself that I didn't care. I was sure my game was better than theirs.

I laughed when I played, because I was having a better time than they were. *Now let them be jealous of me,* I thought. A wonderful new toy appeared in the playroom, a rocking horse. It fascinated me. My horse, however, was not just any horse; it was white and outlined in black with a red wooden seat connecting its sides. My horse was magical and took me anywhere I wanted. On my horse I was the queen, and all the other girls were at my command.

"Hey, you on the monkey bars, come wipe the sweat off my horse," I yelled. "You there on the grass where you're not supposed to be, get over here," I ordered. "My horse has pooped. Clean it up." I once made the mistake of soiling myself while on the rocking horse. After that it was removed it from the playroom, and I never saw it again.

When I was three years old, I took Georgina under my wing. I talked for her, told the nuns when she was hungry, and let them know when she had to go to the bathroom—anything I imagined she wanted. "She needs a blanket.... She's tired.... She wants more chicken.... She wants milk...." I became indispensable, and I hoped Mother S. noticed.

Sometimes I saw children leaving with adults. When I saw people arrive, I rushed to them and said, "Choose me. I'll go with you." If they chose me, I would have to leave my sisters and brothers, but I was willing to do that to leave the orphanage. One sunny day Mother S. called me to her office.

"Beverly, there are two people in my office who would like to talk to you," she said, as met in the hall.

"Yes, Sister."

"They might want you to live with them—so smile, be nice, and be still," she suggested.

"Yes, Sister."

"Remember: behave yourself."

"Yes, Sister."

"Do you have to go to the bathroom?"

"No, Sister." When we entered the room, a couple was sitting to the right.

"Hello, what is your name?" the woman asked.

"My name is Beverly," I answered. "I'm good, I'm smart, I know my colors, I can count, say my ABCs, and I can tie my shoes. I dress myself too, and I'm a good eater. Some kids here cause trouble but not me."

"She is cute, and I believe she's smart," the man said. He took a quarter from his pocket and handed it to me.

"The children aren't allowed to have money," Mother S. said quickly. "They have no place to keep it."

"Are you going to take me with you?" I asked.

"Beverly, that's not polite," Mother S. said sternly. "Go back to the playroom while we talk."

"Yes, Sister. I think you should pick me." They laughed, and Mother S. smiled. Later that day Sister B. told me to go to the office. Mother S. met me there.

"The people who were here like you and want to take you home."

"Are you sure? When am I going?" I asked anxiously. "What should I call them?"

"You will call them mommy and daddy."

"Yes, Sister." I told no one. I knew in my heart I would leave and the other children would stay. Now they would have to wipe the sweat and clean up the poop when my horse pranced back to the playroom. The day I was to leave, my sister Georgina was also leaving. No one had prepared me for this twist. Later I was told by my mother that she and Dad wanted one girl, but Mother S. had called them and explained that I did the talking for Georgina. I was disappointed that I would not be the only child. Obviously I had no say in the matter, so we both left for a new life.

On August 6, 1952, before we left St. Francis, Sister B. took a photograph of our family on the front steps. Connie stood at the top in the center. She wore a yellow and brown dress and looked down at the ground. Tom was to her right, and Alvin was to her left. Ivan and Allen were in front of them. I was on the bottom step with my sisters Georgina and Nancy. We were dressed alike in sky-blue dresses with white-bibbed ruffled fronts. My left hand was clenched in a fist. I wore red socks with brown shoes, which contrasted with my sisters' white socks and white patent leather shoes. After the picture was taken, the rest of my family went inside, while Georgina and I left. There were no hugs from anyone, and I didn't look back. I felt no guilt at the time. As I grew older, though, I often felt I had cheated in getting out and leaving my sisters and brothers behind.

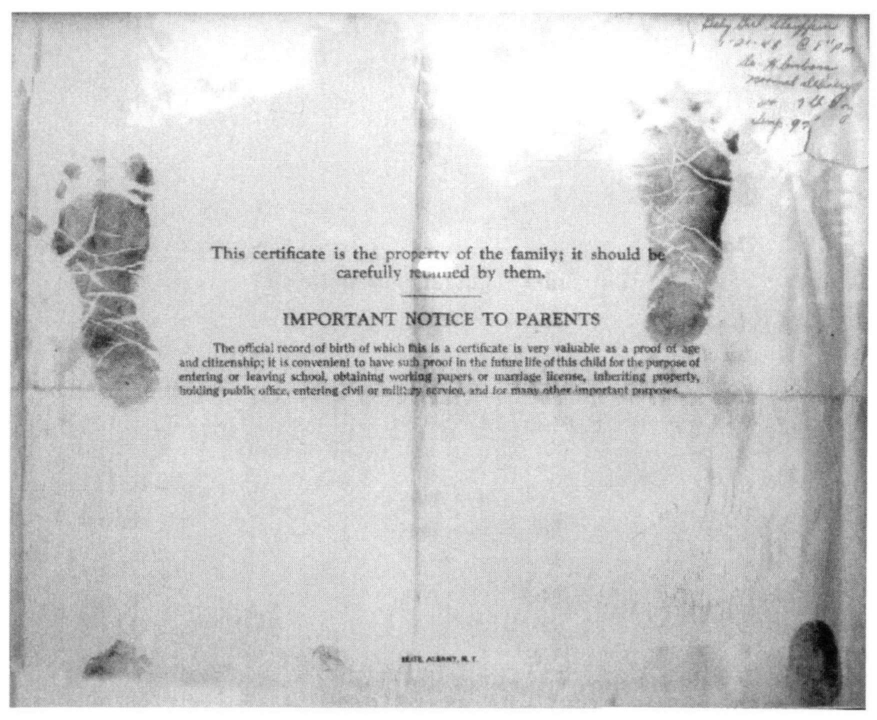

This certificate is the property of the family; it should be carefully retained by them.

IMPORTANT NOTICE TO PARENTS

The official record of birth of which this is a certificate is very valuable as a proof of age and citizenship; it is convenient to have such proof in the future life of this child for the purpose of entering or leaving school, obtaining working papers or marriage license, inheriting property, holding public office, entering civil or military service, and for many other important purposes.

I exist.

Saint Francis Orphanage, Orwigsburg, PA

CHAPTER 2: LIFE ANEW

Julia Trautman, an officer of the Juvenile Court, and her driver Mr. Cuff arrived at the orphanage to transport us to our new home. I'd never been in a car before that I could recall but, nevertheless, had no hesitation. I quickly stepped into the black Chrysler with soft, gray seats, which were so comfortable that I bounced on them; to my surprise, no one corrected me. While I chattered, Georgina slept. Mrs. Trautman, drank from a brown bottle.

"Beverly, why don't you go to sleep like your sister?" she said.

"Because I want to see where we are going."

"You'll only be seeing trees over and over again."

"What if Georgina wakes up?" I asked. "I have to be awake to take care of her."

"I'll watch Georgina. You can go to sleep."

"But I'm not tired."

"OK, but can you be quiet?" *These new people don't know me,* I thought. *I'll tell them it's my birthday, and then they'll give me a present.*

But I can't tell them it's my birthday today; they won't believe me. Maybe Daddy will give me that quarter he offered in Mother S.'s office—he probably has more.

I felt glad that no nuns were traveling with me; they couldn't tell Mommy and Daddy any bad things about me. I promised myself I would be extra good so I wouldn't have to go back. As I looked at the front passenger seat, I noticed the social worker was asleep. The cars, mountains, houses, horses in pastures, and gas stations all passed by. hough the ride took hours, I didn't have enough time to think of more things to tell my parents to ensure my new position in life. Mr. Cuff looked at me in his mirror.

"We're almost there," he said.

"Where?" I said.

"Chelsea, Pennsylvania."

"Chelsea, Pennsylvania?" I'd never heard about that place.

"Yes, at your new house where you will live happily ever after."

"I better wake my sister so she can smile at our new parents too."

"Yes, and I'll wake up Mrs. Trautman."

We turned off the winding, hilly road and approached a long lane. Two ferocious lions standing on their hind legs greeted us from the top of two stone columns. To the left of the lane was a concrete post with a brass sign that read "BELLA VISTA, 1946." To the right there were immense pine trees; one white dogwood was splashed in the center, shading a small part of the right lane. On the left there were rhododendrons, mountain laurels, azaleas, and ferns beneath massive oak and maple trees. An irregular, hilly stone wall formed the border of the grounds. White concrete statues of naked men stood or sat among the trees. One had his elbow on his knee and his fist tucked under his chin. I wanted to know what he was thinking; he looked very smart. Another carried a beautiful silver ball on his shoulder. I thought he must be strong.

We rounded a curve, and like magic a huge house appeared. The house was made of gray and copper sandstone, grouted with cement, with six colonial white wooden pillars supporting it. A multicolored flagstone walkway and porch surrounded the house. The roof was made of red clay tiles in uneven rows topped by a cupola with an eagle weather vane. This grand estate was to be my world for the next thirteen years.

After Mrs. Trautman exited the car, she told us to come out, take her hands, and smile. A beautiful woman with blond hair pulled back stylishly in a bun came out the front door to greet us. She had caring blue eyes, and her lips were bright red. She wore a yellow dress, and I noticed she didn't have a starched bib or a habit that pinched her face; nor did she have rosary beads around her waist with which to hit kids. I liked her right from the start. Just then a gray car pulled up next to Mr. Cuff's car, and a man stepped out. When I saw him stand next to my mother, I realized these were the people I met in Mother S.'s office. I had not been lied to.

My father didn't match my mother's youthful appearance. He was older with gray hair and a bald spot on top. He had a mustache and wore glasses. He wore a gray suit with a navy-blue tie and a red carnation in his lapel, and he was smoking a cigar. He kissed her. This was the first kiss I ever saw. I looked away. This first impression was interrupted when four barking dogs came charging at us from the house. My first memory of dogs was not a good one.

"Don't be afraid," my mother said. "They just make a lot of noise, but they won't hurt you."

"Get…get out of here," my father yelled, kicking at the dogs.

"Joe, stop it," my mother said. "Don't hurt the dogs. You're scaring the girls."

"It's OK, Georgina—they won't hurt you," I said, as I faked courage while mimicking my mother and holding on to her skirt. I knew these people didn't want "fraidy cats," so I continued. "Hi, Mommy and Daddy, this is my sister Georgina. She came along with me."

"Oh, she did, did she?" Mom said, smiling.

"Yes, I take care of her, so I couldn't leave her at the orphanage."

"Well, you both are welcome here," she said. "This is your new home."

"We can stay here?"

"Yes, as long as you behave. Now, let's go inside, and we'll show you around. First I'll show you to the bathroom."

"C'mon, Georgina, hold my hand," I said, holding her with one hand while the other held my mother's. Mother led us to the bathroom.

"This is a bathroom?" I said, looking at the small room. "It only has one toilet and a sink. Where is the bathtub and showers? Where will I take a bath? Where will I go when I have to take a cold shower? Where are the other toilets and sinks? This doesn't smell like a bathroom."

"We have more bathrooms, but they aren't as big as what you know," she responded. "We'll show you around when you're finished using the toilet and washing your hands. You and your sister will have your own bathroom, and it will have a tub and shower."

Mother led us back to the entrance hall, with its floors of Italian marble, naked marble statues, and a gold-inlaid dome with a huge crystal chandelier hanging from the center. A double staircase led to a single set of stairs in the center. The showpiece of the house was an organ, which Dad said had thirteen hundred pipes that were in the attic. A mural was painted above the organ, depicting heaven with half-clad women floating in the sky and cherubs playing harps. I liked what I saw, but I kept my eyes away from the naked statues and looked at the floor when passing them. *The nuns wouldn't approve of these statues,* I thought. *They won't let me stay here if they find out about the naked statues; these people should not allow us to see such nudity.*

"This is big," I said.

"Forty-eight rooms," my father boasted.

"Forty-eight? That's almost fifty." I was amazed.

"The marble floor came from Fiesole, Italy, where my parents lived." He had lost me. My best bet was to smile, and my new parents smiled too. Mrs. Trautman and Mr. Cuff, having freshened up, walked to the car, as my dad handed the social worker a new brown bottle.

"Thanks, Joe," Mrs. Trautman said as she kissed him on the cheek. "I'll let you all get used to each other and will be back in about a month to visit. Be in touch if anything comes up about the girls." They said their good-byes, and I was glad to see them go.

As we walked to the front hall, I saw a girl sitting on a step in the grand staircase. She wore blue silky pajamas looked bigger than us. *Where did she come from?* I hadn't seen her until now. My mother told us her name was Kathleen. She had freckles and red curly hair. She was their nine-year-old daughter, whom they had adopted from St. Francis four years before. I thought she might be visiting and hoped that she didn't live there. If I couldn't be an only child, I at least wanted to be the oldest. Kathleen stared at us.

"I thought they were going to be bigger," she said, sounding disappointed. "I don't want them here." She burst into tears. *We're going to be sent back to the orphanage. I just know it—and all because we are too small.* After a moment that seemed as long as my entire life, my mother put her arms around us.

"They're big enough to play with, Kathleen, and you can be their big sister," my mother said.

"But I wanted them to be my size," Kathleen said, sniffling.

"We can't send them back,'" Mother said firmly. "They're here to stay."Then I knew my mother was the boss, and it didn't matter what Kathleen said. I smirked at her while trying to hold back my own tears. At 6:00 p.m., we ate a dinner of spaghetti and meatballs, salad, and Italian bread. I sat on top of two phone books in a brown leather straight-back chair—one of twenty chairs at the table. A white tablecloth covered the table. At each place was a white linen napkin, sterling silverware, purple stemmed crystal goblets, and china dishes bordered with an ivy-green color with white dogwood flowers. Two vases of flowers graced the table. After dinner my father lit a cigar and blew out the smoke. He looked at me.

"How would you like your name to be Julia?" he asked me.

"I already have a name; it's Beverly," I answered.

"That was your old name. You're at a new place, so you get a new name." I agreed to the new name, and my father explained his reason for choosing that name for me.

"I had a sister named Julia who died when she was twenty-six," he said. I gasped. Now I was afraid I would die when I became twenty-six. He turned to my sister.

"And you'll be Jeannie," he stated. In twenty seconds our former identities vanished; and we were told never to use our former names again, not even as sisters talking to each other.

Kathleen wanted her name changed too. But they told her she'd already had a name change; she used to be Rita. They told us my dad's name was Joe, which I already knew, and my mother's name was also Kathleen. When people spoke about my sister and my mother, they referred to them as Little Kathleen and Big Kathleen.

After dinner, my mother led us upstairs and showed us our room. Jeannie and I were in the suite of rooms next to my mother and father's suite, and Kathleen had her own room across the hall. We had our own bathroom complete with a tub, which also had a shower. And we had our own playroom on the other side of our bedroom. It had no toys, and I missed my horse. My mother bathed us and put our clothes in the trash can.

"But we need our clothes," I protested. "We don't have any other clothes with us."

"We have new ones for you," Mom said. "You'll never have to wear those clothes again."There were two pairs of pajamas on the dresser, and she put them on us.There were no buttons to hold the tops to the bottoms.

"How will these stay on?" I asked.

"Don't worry—they will."

"But there's no buttons to keep our hands out." Mother assured me that was OK.

"Can I wear my button underwear?" I asked. "My undershirt buttons to my pants."

"They're gone. You'll be fine."

She tucked us in, but not tightly, and kissed our foreheads. When she left I went to the bathroom trashcan to retrieve my underwear, but they weren't there. New pajamas, new underwear, and new names all in the same day — that was too much! The next morning we had breakfast: fried eggs, toast, bacon, and jelly. Along with breakfast, we were expected to take vitamins. They smelled awful, and I gagged repeatedly. I was unable to swallow them. "Goddamn it," Father said angrily. "They can't even swallow a pill. Of all the kids in the orphanage, we had to get the dumb ones." I was speechless. Mother S. hadn't prepared me for vitamins. I cried and I was sure we'd be sent back. My father left the room, and Mom tried to console me.

"It's OK, Julia," she explained. He's a doctor and just wants you to be healthy. He thinks a doctor's daughter shouldn't have any trouble swallowing a pill."

I knew that I had disappointed him. I gulped more water but still couldn't swallow the pill. After a couple of more breakfasts like that, they gave up and decided we would get the nutrients we needed through healthy food. My parents soon realized that, if I had something sweet in the morning, I had no trouble eating. They reasoned that eating something was better than eating nothing. So after that my breakfast often consisted of pie, cake, or whatever desserts were left over. Since I talked for Jeannie, I let them know she liked eggs, bacon, orange juice, and only white milk. I saved the chocolate milk for myself, which I made by adding Bosco syrup until the milk turned dark brown.

Dad owned Mercy Hospital, a private hospital in Chester, Pennsylvania, seven miles north of Chelsea. He was a surgeon as well as a general practitioner and was busy most of the day. So we saw him only at breakfast and dinner. He liked that I was a good eater; when I took seconds, and sometimes thirds, he would smile and praise me.

"What an appetite she has," he said to my mother. "She must not have had enough to eat at the orphanage and is trying to make up for it. She must have a hollow leg."

"Hollow leg," I repeated. "What is a *halo* leg? Is that what the saints have over their heads?" He laughed.

"No, it's just an expression. You're so small—where do you put all the food?"

"In my tummy. It must be bigger than my plate." Dad occasionally reminded us that we wouldn't have two or three pork chops if we lived at the orphanage and that we should be grateful that they had adopted us when no one else wanted us.

"We could eat all the food we wanted there," I said. We could eat pretzels and potato chips and cookies as much as we wanted."

"I don't think so, or you wouldn't be eating so much now."

"Stop it, Joe," Mom interjected. Dad inhaled his cigar and blew wonderful crooked circles in the air.

"That's an *o*!" I said in amazement.

"Yes, it is," Dad calmly said. "Come sit on my lap."

"Can you make an *m* for Mommy and a *j* for Jeannie and a *k* for Kathleen?"

"No, just *o*," he replied. I put my finger through one of the *o*'s, thinking Dad had magical powers. Mom served angel food cake with strawberries. As I returned to my seat, I felt a bond with Dad.

When I finished I leaned back in my chair, lifting two legs off the ground. This made Dad angry.

"Julia, stop rocking the chair! I can replace your goddamn head, but I can't replace that chair." His loudness hurt my ears, and his reprimand hurt my feelings. I sobbed and asked to be excused. I ran to the bathroom and cried. The bathroom was a good place to cry because the family respected the privacy of the closed door. And when I turned on the faucets, no one could hear me.

I learned through experience that the music room was farther away from the kitchen and dining room than any other room. It was usually empty and, therefore, a good crying room. I discovered that spaces behind couches and inside closets were also good places to cry alone. I was weak and cried, but I was also strong and hid my weakness. The closets had an additional attraction: I could cry and at the same time hear the adults talk. And so I listened.

Bella Vista, Chelsea, PA

The grand front entrance

Me, Little Kathleen, and Jeannie

CHAPTER 3: THE HELPERS

Three months after we arrived, a couple, Leroy and Alice, came to live with us and help take care of the house, the grounds, and us girls. I had never seen brown skin before we were introduced.

"Are you going to be good for me?" asked Alice.

"No, I'm going to be bad for you," I teased.

Leroy and Alice remained, and between them they assumed the roles of house cleaner, butler, groundskeeper, and chauffer, complete with corresponding uniforms. Standing five feet nine, Leroy had a broad smile. He wiggled his ears without touching them and flared his nostrils at the same time. Though he was an adult, he played with me, which made me smile. He was good at imitating TV characters; he entertained me by saying, "Hey, Poncho. Hey, Cisco," followed by Poncho's laugh. He sang, "Hey, get chure cold beer. Hey, get chure Ballantine." He liked to make up rhymes and encouraged me to rhyme and repeat tongue twisters. I held my tongue and tried saying *black bug's blood* five times. *It's only three words,* I thought. *How hard could it be?* I counted as I spoke: "One—black bug's blood. Two—back bugs bud. Three—block bags blah. Four…wait, let me slow down. Black bug's blood. Five—backs blug bod. There, I did it!" I said triumphantly.

Alice was heavy but moved quickly. She was accurate with the blue plastic flyswatter, which left a hexagonal pattern on our legs. As I matured, I moved faster; as she aged she moved slower. Leroy and Alice had their own living quarters in the basement. Their living room had a stone fireplace; of the three fireplaces in the house, it was the only one that could be lit. Dad often told us fire might fade the Chinese oriental carpets. I enjoyed visiting with Alice and Leroy. In the winter, when we were snowed in and had no electricity, I delighted in roasting hot dogs on sticks. We had marshmallows for dessert; when mine caught fire, I would say I liked them black like that. It was easier for me than admitting a mistake.

When I was eight years old, Leroy took us to the Barnum & Bailey circus in Philadelphia. I sat in the front row, and a clown came to me. He asked me to blow on his nose, and when I did it lit up. I let my guard down and laughed. Leroy also took us to the

Ice Capades. I liked going to these places, but I wished he wouldn't wear his chauffeur's uniform. I felt that other people thought we were better than they were, but I knew differently.

My father's family had been distant, and we had never met them. The unspoken truth was that because we were not "blood family," we weren't "real." Aunt Mary and Uncle Emmett were the exception. Mary was eight years younger than my father. She married Emmett, and they settled in Satsuma, Florida, on the banks of the St. John's River. While building their house in the 1940s, they discovered an Indian burial ground on their property. Aunt Mary preserved many skeletons and Indian artifacts, which she stored in her garage. Their closest neighbor was Edmund Guggenheim, with whom they became lifelong friends. When I was five, Aunt Mary and Uncle Emmett visited us for two weeks. One night at dinner, Uncle Emmett, referred to a political situation while Leroy and Alice were serving dinner.

"If you ask me, I'd say there's a nigger in the woodpile," said Emmett. My parents were horrified. Alice teared up, and Leroy became silent, looking down at the floor as he served the fried chicken and cornbread.

"That's not a word we say here," my father said. Uncle Emmett was embarrassed and apologized to Alice and Leroy, explaining it was a southern expression and never meant as more. "We think you are wonderful folk," Uncle Emmett said.

Neither of my parents was physically affectionate, but Leroy and Alice were. One Saturday morning I was lying on my stomach on the family room floor watching *Howdy Doody*. Just as Buffalo Bob asked, "Hey kids, what time is it?" Alice entered the room. "I know what time it is," said Alice, "It's playtime." And with that I felt Alice's weight on my back bouncing up and down, going faster and faster until she let out a high-pitched squeal. Just then Leroy walked in on her. "Alice, what's the matter with you? Stop doing that to her! That's wrong to do," he yelled. Alice sprang up and bolted from the room with Leroy pursuing on her heels. Though Leroy rebuked Alice for this humping activity in the center of the house, he was also capable of physical affection, but never indoors.

In addition to the house, there were sixteen acres of grounds and woods to attend. There were apple, peach, and pear trees and a large vegetable garden with strawberries to pick, trees to trim, and leaves to rake. There was always plenty of work for Leroy. Mom had her own garden at the top of the hill with a stone wall winding up to it. Her large patch of herbs and vegetables was surrounded by a two-foot stone wall. Strawberry plants were in one section of the garden, and in the rest she planted tomatoes, peppers, onions, and basil. I would help tie the tomato plants to stakes using shreds of old sheets. We walked hand-in-hand to check on the growth, sometimes stopping to eat a ripe tomato. The strawberries were so sweet we never needed sugar.

Leroy cleared the brush and took care of the fruit trees. I liked being outdoors, and I often rode on the tractor or in the Ford pickup, where I sat next to him. When he told me to give him a tummy massage, I would touch him with my hand. I knew it made him feel good, while I felt he was taking care of me.

We kept ordinary thirty-three-gallon trash cans behind the garage where garbage was dumped and emptied. When the cans were full of garbage and maggots, we hauled them across the road to the farmer's pigs. One Saturday while eating lunch in the solarium, I dropped a plate of food on the oriental rug, which made my father furious.

"Do you know how valuable this carpet is?" he shouted. "It's from China. The colors will run. Jesus Christ, what in the hell is the matter with you? How can anyone as smart as you be so goddamn dumb?"

"I didn't mean to," I cried, the tears streaming down. "I'm sorry. I'll get napkins and clean it up."

"That's what pigs do; pigs make messes. You belong with the pigs." Enraged, he called for Leroy.

"Put her in the goddamn garbage can," he ordered. Leroy, the ever-obedient servant, tucked me under his arm and carried me off to the garbage can.

"Don't, don't," I sobbed. "I'll be good. Please, please, please give me another chance," I pleaded. "I promise I'll be good." He lifted the lid of the can and put my head in.

"Stop," I screamed. He lifted me out again and put me down on the ground. I ran to the woods crying.

"Stay outside and let your dad cool down before you go back in," Leroy directed. I didn't come back until after my father drove away.

Lucky me! I had a house, parents, two sisters, and Leroy and Alice, who liked me. I was truly grateful. My parents and other adults praised me for the care I gave Jeannie. I dressed her in the morning, and I awoke in the middle of each night to take her to the bathroom. She was my shadow. She remained silent, and she still pulled on her right earlobe and bit her lower lip out of habit.

Whenever I had a birthday, I wanted Jeannie to get a present as well; not really, but I pretended it was fine with me. On my sixth birthday, my father personally took us shopping. He bought Jeannie a cowboy outfit, complete with boots, a holster, and two guns. For me he purchased a blue cowgirl outfit with fringes, boots, and a rifle. Jeannie was Roy Rogers and I was Dale Evans.

At bedtime I took Jeannie upstairs and lay down with her until she fell asleep. On the nights I didn't fall asleep, I would go downstairs to be with my mother. My dad worked evenings, Alice and Leroy were in their apartment, and Kathleen was in her room, so it was just my mother and me. I would slide my mother's hair-brush from her marble dressing room table and tiptoe to the family room where she watched TV. I would stand behind her, remove the two tortoiseshell combs from her hair, and brush her long golden strands. I believed her hair was gold and related to the Rumpelstiltskin story, in which straw is spun into gold. When my parents had company in the evening, I would sometimes go to the stairs, lean over the interior balcony, and listen to the adults talk. Once I heard them talking about me.

"Julia takes Jeannie to bed every night," my father said.

"Yes," my mother added, "the two of them are inseparable. Jeannie won't do anything without her." Since the conversation was positive, I undressed, tiptoed down the stairs, and drew open the curtains to the formal living room. I appeared naked at the entrance, wearing only a smile. Everyone laughed; I was a big hit. Other times I would put a pillow in my pajamas and pretend I was going to have a baby, which drew more laughs. No one questioned a kid who sought attention in this manner. I learned early on that if the adults were laughing, they couldn't yell.

CHAPTER 4: AND THEN THERE WERE THREE

My mother liked my sister and me; so I thought I should tell her about my sister Nancy, my six year old sister, who remained at the orphanage. I weighed this carefully in my mind. I didn't want to share my mother, but I thought she would like me more if I told her about my sibling. One night after dinner I blurted out to Mom and Dad,

"Did you know I have an older sister named Nancy at the orphanage ?" I blurted out one night after dinner. "I think she would like to be here too." Dad smiled.

"I'm not ready for another child," Mom said looking alarmed.

"Kathleen, Julia truly misses her sister, or wouldn't be mentioning her," Dad responded. My father and I had the last word.

On February 4, 1953, we drove to the orphanage and picked up Nancy, who was six years old. It had been years since she'd been in a car. She became car sick, so, we stopped at a store to buy her a new dress on the way home.

Once back in the car, I thought: *They'll be mad at me because Nancy's sick.Why did she have to get sick today? I've made the wrong decision by talking about her. How am I going to fix this mess? I don't like her anymore.*

On the way home, my father renamed her Rose Marie; we called her Rosie.

"I'm not Rose Marie," she declared. "My name is Nancy."

"No," I quickly said. "You'll live in a house with a new family, and you won't have to wear button underwear." I pulled up my skirt and showed her my underwear with ruffles. "And you get a new name. My name's Julia and Georgina is Jeannie. Our parents are Joe and Kathleen, but we call them Mommy and Daddy."

"Shut up, Beverly," she shot back. "I'm older than you."

"But I was here first," I said, "and I'll help you."

"I don't need your help, Beverly."

"My name is Julia," I reminded her. Still nauseated, she lay down on the seat and slept until we arrived home.

There was an immediate personality clash between her and Mom. Rosie was used to her life and routine at the orphanage where she had been a bright student and gained recognition in the choral group, which sang on a local broadcast every Saturday night. She missed the recognition and the familiarity of these surroundings.

Rosie remembered that my father's sister, Aunt Mary, and her husband, Uncle Amos, had visited the four brothers and one sister remaining at the orphanage. When my mother disciplined Rosie, she usually began by saying, "Why are you not listening to me ? Do you realize that if it had not been for Julia you would never have been here ?You would still be sitting at the orphanage."

Rosie responded, "Aunt Mary and Uncle Amos wanted to adopt me." Rosie responded. "They were coming for me, but you got there first."

"Then why the hell didn't they come for you before we did?" my mother angrily replied. "They had plenty of time."

Rosie could not answer that question. She would glance at me and shout, "Why didn't you just keep your big mouth shut? I was happy at the orphanage."

"I thought you and Mom would like each other," I said. Rosie stormed out of the kitchen and ran outside.

"Julia," Mom said, "with your good memory, I'm surprised you never mentioned Aunt

Mary and Uncle Amos. Do you remember them coming to visit?"

"I don't remember anyone coming to visit us," I said. "There were only nuns there—no regular people."

"Dad and I were told by Mother S. there were no adult family members," Mom said. "I think Rosie invented them to make it seem like she was wanted. She should be thankful she is here."

"I thought I was doing you and Rosie a favor," I said, feeling devastated. "Now I feel badly. I never heard you curse before; I thought only daddies curse."

This was definitely not the successful conclusion I envisioned. My mother was happier before Rosie arrived. Curiously enough, my dad took Rosie's side. I was disheartened because he gave her attention I deserved. I was there first after all. The competition was on. When my parents occasionally went out for dinner, Rosie, Jeannie, and I physically fought. Jeannie never said anything, but she stood up for herself by spitting on us. Rosie's punches left bruises. I punched her back, but it didn't hurt her like she hurt me. My best and only defense was to bite, and I left teeth marks on anyone who picked on me. My parents walked in during one of these fights.

"Jeannie!" Mom screamed. "Spitting is a horrible thing to do. We have germs in our mouths. Don't ever do that to anyone again."

She turned to Rosie and said, "Rosie, you're bigger and stronger than they are. When you punch, you hurt your sisters. Look at Julia's arms," she said, lifting my arm toward Rosie. "Do you see how red they are?"

"And, Julia, I'm surprised at you," she said. "That's not like you. A human bite is worse than any animal bite. Look at the teeth marks you left on Rosie's leg," she said, pointing to Rosie's right calf. "Now, all of you apologize to each other and go to bed."

"Sorry," I said to Rosie, "but you started it."

"I'm not sorry," Rosie said. Jeannie turned her back to Rosie and me and said nothing.

Sometimes when my parents were home, I would tell them my sisters were fighting to get them in trouble. Mom made them sit in a chair, which gave me time to be alone with her.

When I occasionally talked back to Mom, she would put me on a chair in the kitchen for a "time-out." I didn't mind sitting, but staying still bothered me. I would wait until Mom, who was cooking, turned her back, and then I would stand up and try to sit down quickly before she turned back around. If Rosie was in the room, she would say in a high-pitched singsong voice, "Jul-ia is off the chh-aair."

"No, I'm not," I would say and quickly sit down. "Rosie's lying. She's trying to get me in trouble. She wants me to sit longer." And with that Rosie would disappear through the swinging kitchen door.

Little Kathleen was somewhat of a blur after Rosie arrived. She liked to stay clean and dress up; we liked to roughhouse. She was lanky; we were short. She had red curly hair; ours was straight. She liked to clean house; we didn't.

My father had two daughters, Mary and Helen, from a previous marriage. His wife died of tuberculosis when the girls were teenagers. When my father married my mother, both of his daughters were young adults who lived on their own.

My mother was unable to get pregnant, so they adopted Kathleen when she was four and raised her as an only child. In photographs she wears a white fur coat with a matching hat and hand muff. When my parents traveled, she went with them. She seldom got in trouble, and only occasionally did my father have to say to her, "Stop being such a pain in the ass." School was difficult for her, so she was sent to boarding schools until senior high school.

Kathleen was a kind person—an injured animal concerned her—and she would be the one to bring home a stray kitten or nurse a bird until it could fly. One spring she found a blue jay with a broken wing. She carefully placed it in a cardboard box, and she protected it from Tippy the cat by placing the box on the upper outside balcony, which could only be accessed from an interior door. Kathleen made a splint out of gauze and popsicle sticks and fed the bird three times a day from an eyedropper. His wing was on the mend. The big day came where she proudly watched him fly from the balcony to the porch. But alas, the bird flew into the jaws of the waiting cat. Tippy took off toward the woods. Kathleen stormed down the steps and ran out of the house screaming, "Damn you, Tippy. Wait until I get my hands on you."

My mother put her hand on Kathleen's shoulder. "It's only a bird," she said calmly. "There are lots more of them."

Kathleen's feelings were hurt easily as were mine. She too found places to cry alone.

My father immersed himself in his work. He owned Mercy Hospital, with fifty-two-beds, a private hospital in Chester, Pennsylvania. The patient and operating rooms were on the second floor, while three examining rooms, a bathroom, and a kitchen occupied the first floor. In addition the business office and waiting room were on the first floor. A red Coca-Cola machine, with white cursive letters, sat in the waiting room. Cokes were a nickel. It was easy for me to be handed a nickel from any patient who was waiting; or I could run an errand knowing I would get a nickel.

For a period of time, my sister Mary, my father's daughter from his first marriage, had her pediatric office and reception room on the first floor. She was known as Dr. Mary, and she was the first female graduate of Hahnemann Medical School in Philadelphia.

When I was six, I became Dr. Mary's patient. Mom brought me into her examining room, and Mary lifted me onto the table and pulled down my ruffled panties.

"That redness is what concerns me," Mom said. "She keeps telling me how it hurts when she pees."

"Someone's been messing with her," said Dr. Mary while turning to Mom. Mary pulled up my panties and gave me a lollipop for being so good. She led me to the play table and handed me a magazine, *Highlights for Children*, in which I searched for the hidden objects. Later when Mom told Dad of Mary's exam, he said, "Bullshit. Julia just drinks too much Coca-Cola. The soda has acid in it, and that's what is affecting her." Years later I realized soda doesn't cause vaginal infections; Dad's cursed reaction had been his defense.

My mother was the hospital administrator, business manager, and personnel director, though she had no titles for the work she did. I enjoyed the days when I went with her and sat at an adjoining desk, hunting and pecking away for hours on the typewriter.

I had another hospital experience one Saturday night during the summer. My parents didn't go out often, but one night they took

Kathleen and Rosie to the opera. Lucy Hyers, the night-shift nurse at the hospital, watched Jeannie and me. Mom and Dad were supposed to pick us up when the opera was over. Mrs. Hyers wanted to sleep; so she gave us a sedative, phenobarbital, which put us to sleep.

I woke with a start in the middle of the night. The room was dark. I went to the window and saw a fire in the distance. I had a hard time breathing. My arms and hands were flapping. I was sure the whole city was on fire and that my parents were burning in it. I crawled back to the bed and leaned against the wall. I watched Jeannie sleep peacefully as I raced back and forth to the window to check on the fire. I knew I had to stay awake in case the fire got closer and I had to lead her to safety. My body was covered with mosquito bites, and I scratched my arms.

As a kid I had severe reactions to mosquitoes, and it was common in the summer to have bites all over me. They itched ; I *had* to scratch them, causing them to bleed and form scabs. I knew I should give them time to heal, but when my fears of abandonment were aroused, I would scratch them open and suck the blood to soothe myself.

This reaction occurred summer after summer into adulthood. Mom insisted I leave the bites alone, and she would spank me if there was blood on my socks, sleeves, or bed clothing indicating that I had scratched them open. I discovered that if I sucked the blood until it was dry, I didn't leave evidence. Then I would wear slacks or long-sleeve shirts. Eventually the older bites would heal, but new ones replaced them.

The night of the fire, I scratched all my mosquito bites open. The blood was too much to control by sucking; so I blotted the blood with my pillowcase. I bled on the sheets and took them to the hospital operating room, where I stuffed them in the laundry chute. Once again I thought I did a bad thing by bleeding on the sheets. I fell asleep exhausted from crying.

When I awoke at dawn and looked out the window, I realized the fire had been in the incinerator. The sedative and its hallucinatory effects had worn off. I woke Jeannie and took her to the bathroom. Then I woke Mrs. Hyers.

"Where's Mommy and Daddy?" I asked. "They didn't come to pick us up."

"Yes, they did, but you were both asleep, so they let you stay overnight. They'll be here soon."

I felt better. They hadn't burned up after all. I didn't tell anyone what had happened that night. No one noticed my matted hair or the dark circles under my eyes. It felt good to go home, where nobody knew I had messed up the hospital sheets.

Rosie, Me, Jeannie and Kathleen being splendid in the grass.

CHAPTER 5: QUALITY TIME

My father had a busy schedule. He was a general practitioner as well as a surgeon; so he had limited time away from work. In addition to the hospital and his office, he was the prison physician and the coroner's physician. He occasionally made house calls, and sometimes urgent cases would visit to our home.

As the coroner's physician, Dad was called to go to funeral homes, where he performed autopsies on any suspicious deaths or anyone not under a physician's care. He began his day at 6:00 a.m. and came home for a short nap and dinner before returning to his office for the evening. When he went to funeral homes to perform autopsies, I would wait with my mother for his return.

Saturday and Sunday afternoons he watched television; baseball, football, or an old movie—and I watched with him. My mom and sisters disliked sports; so this was my one-on-one time with Dad. He didn't like it when I disrupted his concentration with questions, but being with him was incentive to be quiet.

One Saturday afternoon he received a call from an undertaker. My mother was sick, so he took Jeannie, Rosie, and me with him. As his black Cadillac idled, he unwrapped a Septimo cigar. My sisters and I watched as he discarded the paper band in the front passenger seat. If two of us sat in the front, we usually scrambled for the ring—the lucky one had a new ring. He lit up, and we were on our way. His car smelled stuffy with the smoke from his cigar.

When we arrived, Dad took us in to watch him perform the autopsy. He didn't prepare us for what we would see—no pictures, no explanations. The undertaker and Dad exchanged greetings. "Kathleen's sick, so I brought the girls along," he said, looking down at the three of us standing by his side. "Girls, this is Mr. Videon." Mr. Videon asked our names and excused himself to his office.

We continued walking to the autopsy room. Dad opened the door and turned on the bright light, which was centered over a corpse covered by a white sheet and lying on a gurney. A pungent odor stung my nose. "Oooh yuck, what is that awful smell?" I asked.

"That's embalming fluid," Dad said. "It's used to keep the body from rotting like dead animals do in the woods."

Dad pulled the sheet off with one quick motion revealing a naked woman. I was embarrassed, and I wondered how she might feel about strangers viewing her. The nude marble statues and paintings at home were nothing like the sight of this naked corpse.

Jeannie and I focused on her pink plastic hair curlers, trying to look away from her body, while Rosie watched Dad. He placed his black bag on the table near the woman's head and reached into it for his instruments.

"This is a scalpel," he said, holding it up. "It's very sharp, and I use it to cut through skin."

"Skin is thin," I said. "I can cut through it with my nails or teeth."

Ignoring my comment, Dad continued. "Under the skin we'll find muscles and tissues."

"Like Kleenex?" I asked. He gave me a disgusted look.

I didn't watch the incision, but Rosie did. "Here are her heart, lungs, and stomach," he told her, pointing to each organ. Dad was pleased with Rosie's attention and smiled.

"I want to see all this stuff too," I blurted out. He sat me on a white metal stool behind him so I could see his work. I looked but later couldn't remember what I saw.

Dad seemed proud that Rosie helped him sew the woman up. At home he told Mom that someday Rosie will probably be a doctor. When the woman was being sewn up, I was surprised to see how easily Dad's rounded needle, with its thick black string, went through her skin. It was as if the skin were as thin as the pink dotted Swiss material of the new dress Mom had made for me.

I listened for the phone to ring on weekends, and I could hear my father's end of the conversation. If it sounded like he had to perform an autopsy, I would park myself at the back door and ask him if I could go. When he said yes, I felt special. I pulled one over on my sisters and got to be with Dad while they were home riding horses.

One Sunday morning I saw a man's body in three sections on the guerney. "Damndest thing," Dad said to Mr. Nacrelli, the undertaker.

"Yeah, and he's a professor at Swarthmore College," Mr. Nacrelli said. "He tied himself to the railroad tracks. I guess he was serious about dying."

"Amount of education has nothing to do with the depths of despair," Dad said.

Another time I saw a three-year-old boy who had drowned in the river and was found after three days, blue and swollen. *He's about my size*, I thought—*that could be me lying there*. Dad measured him with a tape measure. The little boy was thirty-six inches long just like me. But I was seven years old. I hoped my father wouldn't cut him open. *If he does all that water will squirt out on me.* Since the cause of death was apparent, fortunately, Dad didn't have to cut him open. On the way home, Dad was silent in the car. That was fine with me because I was spending time with him. I hoped he was proud of me and would tell Mom I was going to be a doctor. He didn't.

CHAPTER 6: THE WONDER OF ACHIEVEMENT

When I was four years and eight months old, I entered kindergarten at St. Anthony's Catholic School in Chester, Pennsylvania. The school was five blocks from the hospital. My mother drove Kathleen and me to school, while Jeannie stayed home with Alice. At lunch we would walk to the hospital from school, where Big Pearl, the hospital head cook, greeted us and served us at the kitchen table reserved for the help. Her smile was as big as her girth. If I didn't like what was on the hospital menu, she would ask me what I wanted. My wants consisted of four items: a can of Campbell's chicken noodle soup, a box of frozen spinach, a mustard sandwich, or a raisin bread and ketchup sandwich. I usually stuck with one item for a week before switching to another..

After lunch, while walking back to school, we passed Lavella Brothers produce, Pileggi Builders, Zapala Realty, and LaSpada hoagie shop. Mom picked us up after school, and we would travel the ten miles home arguing about who was going to sit by the window. Over time the window seat became more prized over time with the advent of the push button. The passenger in the front seat controlled the airflow. If I sat there, I could allow more or less air depending on how I was getting along with those in the back seat. Whoever sat up front did the same thing.

When I learned to read in first grade, a new world opened for me. I enjoyed reading, and the adults expressed approval. Mom was proud of me; the nuns marveled at me; and Dad bragged to others about me.

School also brought negatives. I got in trouble in first grade for not being with the rest of the class in our reading workbooks. While everyone followed on page sixteen, I was on page thirty-three. Harry, a classmate, raised his hand and said, "Sister Amelia [our first grade teacher], Julia's not on the same page as we are, and she's working ahead." The teacher stood me in front of the class for the rest of the reading lesson so I wouldn't work ahead. I felt shame.

The first time I stayed after school involved the pencil sharpener. It was gray—the kind which had a handle to turn and a small container that held the shavings. As you emptied the sharpener, you could smell the musty aroma of lead and trees. One day the sharpener broke. Anyone who needed to sharpen a pencil had to go to the closet and use a small handheld sharpener. The pencil was inserted into the hole, and the shavings would fall into the trash can.

I was caught in the act! My first-grade boyfriend, Alex Herman, and I went in the closet at the same time and shut the door. Another boy came into the closet and saw us kissing. He immediately reported us to Sister Amelia. Alex and I stood in front of the class for the rest of the day. I didn't know kissing was wrong, but I did know the other kids looked at me and laughed. I hung my head the entire time. When our mothers came to pick us up, we had to tell them what we had done. Sister Mary Amelia made a big deal of it, but my mother seemed to think it was innocent.

Another day my older sister told Mom I was chasing boys at recess. That was the first time—but not the last—that I heard my mother say I was "boy crazy."

One day in second grade, I was running during recess. I rounded a corner, and suddenly everyone disappeared. I was in a dark hole!

I was scared, but I was able to move in the dark and felt something scamper over my feet. I heard someone call my name, and I looked toward the voice. A light shone on me, and I could see concrete steps. The voice told me to climb the stairs. The front of my legs were scraped and bleeding, but Mother Mary Emerencia, the principal, didn't seem to notice. She scolded me for causing the cellar door to cave in since I wasn't supposed to be on it in the first place. She made me go to all eight classrooms and show the other children what happens when you don't listen. Sister Mary Mel, my second grade teacher, cleaned me up.

The other kids know I'm bad, and they stay away from me so they won't get in trouble. Once again, I saw the invisible wall with them on one side and me on the other. I enjoyed playing by myself, smiling the entire time.

Second grade was wonderful. Sister Mary Mel liked my stories, and every day after lunch I stood in front of the class—but this time it was to tell them a story. Then she would send me to the seventh-grade classroom to retell my stories. Everyone applauded me there, and Sister Mary Abraham, the seventh grade teacher, sent me up and down the rows so her students could give me candy and pennies as payment for my stories.

One of my stories included my brothers and sisters. I told the class that when I became an adult, I would look for the rest of my family so we would all be together. I never mentioned this to my parents. By that time it was clear they were my family, and I didn't dare hurt my mother's feelings by talking about my brothers and sister.

Sister Mary Mel told my story to my mother when she came to pick me up. It was clear that Mom's feelings were hurt. "Why did you tell others about your 'real' family?" she asked on the ride home.

"I didn't," I said.

"According to Sister Mary Mel, you told a story to the class and said you wanted to find your 'real' family when you were an adult. Mom glanced at me and continued, "Julia, you're very ungrateful. You should get down on your knees every day and thank God we adopted you when no one else wanted you." Obviously she was angry.

"Mom, I was only telling a story," I explained. "I wouldn't even know how to find them," I cried. "I know you and Dad are my family, and I'm thankful you adopted me." I wiped my tears on my sleeve.

Now I was confused. I thought it was safe to share this "secret" in school, where my parents wouldn't find out, but Sister Mary Mel told on me. I wanted to be loyal to my adoptive parents, yet I didn't want to forget the brothers and sister I had left behind. I never mentioned my siblings to anyone again, but I kept that thought in the back of my mind for the future and for imaginary play.

On the last day of school, Sister Mary Mel asked me to remain in the classroom. When the other children left, she gave me a small figurine of an angel on bended knee dressed in blue. I felt special because she had singled me out. Then she told me to hide it so no one else would know. She didn't want the other kids to feel slighted that she hadn't given one to each of them. I wanted to show the other children to let them know that Sister Mary Mel liked me better, but I told no one at school.

I brought it home and told Rosie, who said, "That's not worth anything. Nuns have lots of those statues." When I awoke the next morning, I found the statue in a zillion bits and pieces on top of my dresser. In the back of my mind, I thought of Rosie, but perhaps the cat had knocked it down in the middle of the night. Who's to say?

One day on the playground, a group of other seven-year-old girls came up to me and asked, "Why don't you have real parents? Why did your real parents give you away?" They took me by surprise, but I quickly thought of an answer. "My parents didn't give me away," I said. "They were killed in a car crash. I was with them and saw them die. Both my legs were broken, and that's why I'm so short. My father I have now was the doctor who took care of me, and that's how I came to live with him and my mom."

I didn't feel the pain of that experience until years later. Those girls viewed me as different, but they had sympathy for me and didn't ask again. I didn't know the true story of my birth parents at that time, but I was sure whatever it was could not have been helped. I told myself that my parents didn't want to give me away and that when I grew up I would find out the story. I would never admit it to anyone, but secretly I suspected they gave me away because I was bad.

In third grade I assumed I could go to the seventh-grade class and tell stories like I had done the previous year. On the first day of school, I went on my own to the upper class. I told a story about television and the little girl who thought real people lived inside her TV. In the midst of my tale, a messenger entered the room and gave Sister Mary Abraham a note from my third-grade teacher, Sister Mary Victor. I was told immediately to go to my classroom—no ending of my story, no pennies, no candy.

I began reading more. I would take a book to recess and sit in a corner of the building and read while others played. I usually did well with exams, and in the spring we took the Archdiocese of Philadelphia's annual exams. I had thirty-five minutes to work on the grammar section, which was a breeze. I finished first. Sister Mary Victor scanned the papers as they were passed to the front, and then her olive-skinned face was suddenly in front of me. Her brown eyes widened; she raised her dark bushy eyebrows; and she looked at me with rage.

She pinched my cheek firmly and said, "Why didn't you listen to me? You were supposed to circle the subjects and underline the predicates, and you did just the opposite. Erase the whole page and start again."

While I sat crying and erasing, my classmates went to recess. The mixture of the tears and erasures left smudges and holes on my paper. Sister Mary Victor tore my paper in half in front of everyone and gave me a zero. I couldn't tell anyone at home about my failure.

In fourth grade I carefully followed Sister Mary Christopher's directions. I wanted to get 100 percent on all of my work, so I would check and recheck papers before handing them in. I walked quietly down the aisle to Sister's desk. "Excuse me, Sister," I whispered, "I don't mean to bother you, but I want to make sure I'm doing this page correctly."

"Yes, Julia," she said. "You always do a nice job—it's not necessary to ask me about each workbook page."

I returned to my seat, put my head down, folded my hands in prayer, and waited patiently for the other kids to finish. After the papers were passed to the front of the class and Sister had marked them, she would announce the grades. I knew I wasn't the smartest student in the class. There were two or three girls who always earned perfect scores, but in my mind I put them on one side of my invisible wall and me on the other. I was sure they thought they were better than me; so I decided I wouldn't talk to them again.

One afternoon Anthony received a 70 percent on a test, and when Sister told the class, he shouted, "Damn you!" The other students looked at him and then at Sister. "Anthony, what did you say?" she asked, matching his tone.

"Damn you," he repeated. "My dad says that when he's mad at my mom or us kids."

"Come to the front of the class," Sister said. We thought Sister was going to hit him across his mouth with her ruler. Instead, she opened her top drawer, pulled out a small bar of soap, and placed it on her desk. She skimmed the top of it with her scissors and placed bits of soap on his tongue. "That's for having a dirty mouth," she said.

"Soap?" I said aloud. "I like the taste of soap."

"Well, Julia," she said, "then you may have some too." And with that she walked up the aisle to my desk. I opened my mouth willingly.

"It's not Ivory," I said, "but it's good." After that incident the soap wasn't needed again.

I did well in all subjects except handwriting. No matter how hard I tried, I just couldn't make the letters look like the ones I saw in our *Palmer Method* book. I attempted to copy the spirals, but they spiraled either up or down the page. I looked at the papers of other students around me and saw that their papers looked much like the sample. I traced over and over again, but mine was always smudged and sloppy. Because I felt ashamed of my lack of ability, I hid my paper by curving my hand around it so the other kids couldn't see.

One day I was called to the fifth-grade classroom. *They're going to skip me a grade*, I immediately thought. But to my surprise, my sisters Jeannie and Rosie were standing in front of the class. Sister Mary Francis instructed me to stand between them.

"Boys and girls, look at this," she said as she held the card to the class. "Rose Marie returned her report card, and my signature was obviously damaged."

Then she turned to me. "Did you trace over my name, Julia?" she asked.

"No, Sister, I didn't do that. I don't know how to write like you," I said.

She looked at Jeannie and asked, "Did you do this?"

"No, Sister."

Then she got in Rosie's face. "That leaves you as the culprit. Why did you distort my signature?"

"Honest, I didn't."

Though Sister Mary Frances was relentless in her questioning, none of us owned up to the tracing. Since the interrogation was going nowhere, she tried a different tactic. "Look how sloppy you are, Julia. Your shoelaces are untied, and your socks are around your ankles."The class laughed at me, and I cried. Jeannie joined in. Rosie cried because she was being accused of something she didn't do.

"Look at the three crybabies," she said to the class, which elicited more laughter. Finally she said, "I know which one of you did it," and she let Jeannie and I return to our classes.

My class was in the middle of penmanship practice. I joined in and did the exercises, sniffling as tears ran down my cheeks. I hadn't tried to intentionally distort Sister Mary Frances's handwriting. I just thought it was so perfect and beautiful—I wanted to trace hers so that maybe I could make mine look nice too.

When Rosie came home, she was angry at Jeannie and me because Sister had blamed her and smacked her hands . Afraid of Rosie's wrath, I stood staunch in my denial, and she never found out I was to blame.

In the spring of fourth grade, the class prepared for the sacrament of confirmation. We had to choose a middle name that was the name of a saint, who would then serve as our model and protector. I picked Mary, after the Blessed Virgin Mary, mother of God. She was the highest-ranking woman in the Bible, I reasoned. I was attracted to her purity, and she always wore blue, which was my favorite color. Jeannie thought Lulu would be a good middle name, but Mom told her there was no Saint Lulu.

Each child was required to have an adult sponsor who attested to his or her commitment to Catholicism. The sponsor sat in the pew next to the candidate. My parents chose Julia Curran, the social worker who had taken us from the orphanage to our house, as my sponsor.

In our daily religion class, we studied the two hundred questions and answers from the Boston Catechism. To my absolute delight, we had a second religion class for confirmation. This class replaced handwriting. I practiced the questions and answers at home as well as in school.

The first question and answer was "Who made us? God made us." The succeeding questions had longer answers. While handwriting was my weakness, memorization was my strength.

Sister Mary Christopher informed us that the archbishop of the diocese of Philadelphia would administer the sacrament. "The archbishop is a very holy man in the church," she said. "There are priests, monsignors, bishops, archbishops, cardinals and the pope. The archbishop is an emissary of the pope, and he is referred to as Your Excellency. He will select the questions and point to any one of you to answer," she explained. "If you don't respond exactly as written, you will be denied confirmation in front of the entire congregation."

The big day came. We looked pure in our white dresses and white suits. We walked single file with the boys on the right side of the aisle and the girls on the left. As we reached the front of Saint Anthony's Church, we crossed in front of the altar where the archbishop sat on a throne. He was dressed regally in gold vestments and a gold miter. We continued our procession and filled the pews.

The archbishop explained the sanctity of the day and asked a few easy questions, but he did not call on me to answer any of them. *I know every one of these questions by heart. I know the exact words of the seven deadly sins, the seven gifts of the Holy Ghost, the eight beatitudes, and the twelve fruits of the Holy Ghost. I didn't study so hard not to be asked anything.*

In closing the archbishop said, "My children, I am satisfied that you are all worthy of confirmation. Is there anything I have forgotten?" he asked. My hand shot up, and my sponsor nudged me with her leg. "Shhh," she whispered.

"Yes, Your Excellency, you forgot to ask us which are the twelve fruits of the Holy Ghost." The silence of the church was broken by quiet guffaws.

"Well, I didn't think anyone would know them," the archbishop said as he glanced around the church.

"I do," I said immediately. "The twelve fruits of the Holy Ghost are charity, joy, peace, patience, benignity, goodness, long-suffering, mildness, faith, modesty, continence, and chastity."

"Well done," he said with a smile.

Then he washed his hands and recited a prayer. Each of the children knelt in turn before the archbishop, who addressed us by our chosen confirmation name. I felt happy as he placed his right hand on my head and anointed me with the holy chrism oil; not all my studying had been in vain.

My parents were busy attending a reception for a newly elected judge rather than my confirmation. But the following day Dad received a call from Monsignor John Zazzara from Saint Anthony's, who told him the archbishop was impressed and wanted to know who that little girl was. Dad was proud of me for speaking up.

CHAPTER 7: THE RETURN OF THE NUN

One summer day in my ninth year, Mom announced we would be having special dinner guests. Generally, she cooked Italian cuisine well, though she was Irish-American. She took lessons from my father's mother, Philomena, who was Italian. On any given Sunday, we would have anywhere from four to twenty guests. Whoever dropped by was always invited to stay for dinner. Homemade spaghetti sauce cooked for two days was the base. Veal scaloppini, chicken cacciatore, braciola, rigatoni, or lasagna were accompanied by garlic bread and a salad. The food was plentiful. Sometimes there were so many people that we had a table for kids in the kitchen, while the adults ate in the dining room.

When the door bell rang, I answered the door and was met by six nuns who looked vaguely familiar. They were from the orphanage. There was a convent for retreats a few miles from our house, and they were spending two weeks there. They had previously contacted my parents and were invited for dinner.

"Do you remember me?" Sister Bartholomew asked.

"Yes, I remember you," I said cautiously. "I live in this big house now. I can read and do arithmetic and get a good report card." I paused to take a breath. "And I set the table and have good manners."

Sister B. smiled. "We're visiting in the area, and your parents invited us for dinner," she assured me. "May we come in?"

My mother appeared at the entrance, welcomed everyone, and introduced us. While the adults conversed in the formal living room, I sorted through papers in my school bag, and selected the marks of ninety or above to show to the nuns. They were impressed and continued their conversation about the retreat.

"We'll pray often and have hours of silence," Sister B. said. "And we have a pool where we can swim."

"Swimming! With all your clothes on?" I asked. "How will you do that?" I imagined their rosary beads floating with their habits and bibs. "I can swim," I added. "How will you lift your arms over your head?"

"Julia, stop asking so many questions," my mother interrupted. "You're being rude."

"It's OK," Sister Bartholomew said with a smile. "It's hard for people to imagine us in swimsuits."

Just then Leroy rang the dainty dinner bell.

We took our places at the table, and my father showed the nuns to their seats. I looked around the table admiringly at the crystal, sterling silver, and china. The two candelabras placed off-center on the table were lit. Mom asked Rosie to say grace.

I looked down the hall and saw Alice and Leroy approaching with fried chicken, cornbread, mashed potatoes, and green beans. Because Sunday was usually Italian day at home, I was expecting Italian cuisine.

"Is this all we're having?" I said, disappointed.

"All we're having!" Sister Bartholomew exclaimed. "Julia, this is a wonderful meal. You never had meals like this in the orphanage."

"But this is Sunday, and that's Italian day," I replied. "I was looking for spaghetti as well."

"Maybe you have forgotten the orphanage and would like to go back with us," Sister Bartholomew. said.

I looked into her eyes and said, "Yes, that would be nice."

"OK, we'll take you back with us then."

As coffee and apple pie were served, I excused myself from the table, went to the family room, and hid behind the bar under the sink. When the nuns were ready to leave, Mom called for me. I didn't answer, and I heard Rosie singing: "Julia's going back to the or-phan-age. Julia's going back to the or-phan-age." Mom spotted me and said, "It's time to go; I packed your bag."

"I don't want to go," I said in a trembling voice. "I want to stay here."

"All right, you can stay, but in the future, don't say things like that. It hurt my feelings."

The nuns left, and I stayed.

CHAPTER 8: THE DISCOVERY

Because Dad had performed an autopsy on a teenager who had drunk alcohol, he allowed us to drink beer at home. He reasoned that this would deter us from sneaking it later while in an automobile, thus avoiding any accidents. He also thought the yeast and hops were healthier for us than Coca-Cola. It wasn't unusual for my sisters and me to enjoy one or more bottle of beer while watching our favorite television shows—such as *Howdy Doody*, *Pinky Lee*, or *Fury*—on a Saturday morning. The beer tasted better than either soda or milk.

Dad complained more than once that he couldn't find a beer in the refrigerator. So as soon as I heard his car pull into the driveway, I would put a couple beers on the top shelf from the vegetable bin where I had hidden them. Homework in the evening was frequently accompanied by a beer or two. Rosie, Jeannie, and I often competed for that last one.

By age ten I didn't care if my beer was cold or not. I would pour it over ice. Occasionally Mom told us we were too young to be drinking and to stop. So we learned to wait to drink our beers until she went to the market or when she was cooking. When we heard her approach the family room, we would stuff the beer bottles between our bodies and the seat cushions.

Dad always ordered ten cases of beer at a time, so it was easy for me to remove the two cases from the top and help myself to several bottles from the third case. Before I rushed to my room, I would put the two cases back on top. I had special hiding places for beer, such as under my pillow, beneath the bed, or in my dresser. To cover my tracks, I would volunteer to load the refrigerator, which Mom appreciated.

Dad also stored alcohol in a walk-in whiskey closet in the basement that was always locked. I kept my eye on the worn, brown, cracked leather key case, which was hidden in various places. While everyone else was busy, I managed to find the key whenever I needed it. The shelves on the right and left sides of the closet were stocked with all shapes, sizes, and colors of bottles. The green stuff was good and so were the dark-red and pink wines. I didn't like the clear liquids. When I noticed the alcohol level sinking, I added water. More thrilling than the taste of the liquor was the notion that this was my secret, and I wasn't about to share it with anyone.

In my teen years, I would invite five or six girls over for a slumber party on a night when Leroy and Alice were away. I always made sure I knew where the keys were and would retrieve them late at night. One snowy evening Beth, Joan, Daisy, and Rita arrived for a sleepover. We passed time in the evening eating pizza, styling each other's hair, and painting our nails, each a different color. Daisy brought her 45 rpm records along that included "Teen-Angel," "The Lion Sleeps Tonight," and "Leader of the Pack." We sang hearty choruses of "Does Your Chewing Gum Lose Its Flavour (On the Bedpost Overnight?)" and "Henry the Eighth." Finally, when all was quiet upstairs, I put my finger to my lips. "Sh," I whispered. "It's important to be quiet so we don't wake anyone—follow me single file."

We tiptoed across the hall, and I unlocked the closet door. "Wow!" Beth said as I flipped on the light. "Look at all the bottles of wine, whiskey, and cordials. Your father has his own state store."

"Cordial?" I asked. "What's a cordial - is that a friendly drink?"

"A cordial is syrupy liquor that people drink after a special dinner," Daisy explained. She pointed to the shelf on her left. "Like that crème de menthe or Drambuie or anisette. People pour cordials in a small glass and sip it slowly while smoking cigars and cigarettes."

"We have little glasses under the bar upstairs," I said. "I'll go get five, and then let's get cordial." Beth offered to go with me, but I declined. "Everyone stay here. I'll be right back."

I found the glasses, but they were dusty, so I washed and dried them. When I returned several bottles were already opened, and tasting had begun without me. "Taste this," said Rita. "It smells like licorice."

"Mm, this one tastes like cherries," said Joan as she smiled and passed the bottle to Beth.

"Let's sit in a circle," I suggested. "We'll each pick a different bottle we think we'd like, fill our glasses, and then pass it on. The only rule is that you have to drink at least half a glass, even if you don't like the smell."

Triple sec became unbelievably funny. "That must mean it makes you want to have sex three times," said Rita as she passed her glass to the left.

"I know what it means," Joan said. "Adults drink it when they are having sex with three people." And with that, unstoppable giggling began. About an hour later, Rita looked pale;

Daisy tripped over her words; Joan and Beth were bumping into each other's shoulders; and I was trying to make sense of it all. "I think you should all go to the bedrooms," I slurred. I saw them out, turned off the light, locked the door, and stumbled up the stairs to return the keys to the barroom drawer. The only traces of evidence in the whiskey closet were the opened bottles and five sticky cordial glasses.

The basement was strangely quiet when I returned. I walked to the bedrooms, but they were empty. Then I heard sounds of glee and looked out the window of the back door. My friends were in the yard. Rita was puking in the snow, and Joan, Daisy, and Beth, clad only in their pajamas, were making beautiful snow angels. I impulsively joined them.

What the girls didn't know, and what I had not cared about, was that we were being creative in a part of the yard that was under my parents' bedroom. From out of nowhere, spotlights shone on us, and we scampered back to the safety of indoors. Rita was already in bed, and the rest of us stayed quiet in the dark, eventually falling asleep.

Soon after my party, Dad stopped stocking the whiskey closet. He bought a couple bottles of scotch, which he kept in the kitchen. When he watched TV on Saturday or Sunday afternoons, I would volunteer to make him his scotch and water on the rocks. I filled the tumbler to allow sips for me. As time went on, my sips became gulps, and I would return to the kitchen to refresh his drink. I enjoyed being his personal barmaid and watching TV on the weekends. This was part of our one-on-one time that wasn't available during the week.

The limited amount of time I saw Dad was precious. When he didn't arrive home on time, I worried that something had happened to him. He often had to work late, and I would worry. If there was a severe storm, I just knew that he had been struck by lightning. If the roads were covered with snow, I was certain he had slid off the road and was killed.

We wouldn't eat dinner until Dad came home from his afternoon office hours. In anticipation of his arrival, I would go to the music room and play the piano, thinking how nice it would sound to him when he arrived. If he still hadn't shown up after fifteen minutes had passed, I feared he had died. I would lie down on the French provincial gold silk couch and cry and suck on my arm until it was bruised. If I heard anyone approach the room, I would pretend to be asleep so no one could tell I was crying. Finally I would hear him come home, and everything was great. *Thank goodness he's OK*, I thought. *Mom will be happy too*. I would hurry to the kitchen to greet him but stop short. I knew this was his time with Mom. I would watch them kiss, and I knew everything was OK in this world—they were both there.

If they went out for the evening and didn't return at the expected time, I became concerned. I would lie in my bed and watch the shadows on my wall created by the headlights of passing cars, hoping each passing car was theirs. Finally, when I saw the lights, I would jump out of bed, go to the window, and watch them pull into the lane. Relieved, I would return to bed so they wouldn't know I was up past my bedtime. They were never aware that I was anxiously awaiting their return.

CHAPTER 9: RELATIVES

Though I never met my grandparents on my father's side, I knew my grandparents on my mother's side. They watched us occasionally when Alice and Leroy were off duty. They either stayed with us at our house or watched us at their apartment on in Chester.

My grandad was a tall, lanky man with white hair and a permanently stern look on his face. He always wore khaki shirts and trousers and high-top black boots. My mother told me he was strict when she was a child. He was especially harsh with her brothers, Joe and Jack, demanding they be seen and not heard. He was Irish, while my grandmom, whose maiden name was Simpson, was English and maintained her English accent.

Grandmom was petite with short, wavy white hair and blue eyes. She usually wore an apron and liked to bake. She smiled more than Grandad, but not too often. I was intrigued by her bowed legs, which were not to be mentioned. I never liked her, but I tolerated her for my mother's sake. Grandmom made it obvious she favored my cousins since they were blood related and hence "real" family.

Mom told me, that when she was born, Grandmom was disappointed because she had only wanted boys. Two years after Mom's birth, Grandmom had Jack, who was her favorite. Mom often told Dad she was probably the best thing that ever happened to Grandmom since Dad employed Grandad at the hospital as a maintenance man. Dad also helped them out financially by paying the rent for their apartment.

While vacationing in June 1956, Grandad died from a sudden heart attack. My parents brought Grandmom to our house, where she stayed in the guest room. We didn't learn of his death until the next morning. Mom told us, "Go to Grandmom and tell her you're sorry, but don't stay too long."

I brought along my toy panda bear I had won the day before at the annual hospital fete. I knocked at her door. "Yes," she said feebly.

"It's Julia, may I come in?" I asked as I entered.

I went to the left side of her bed, and she rolled toward me. "Mom told me Grandad died," I said. "I'm sorry. Here, would you like my new panda bear?" I offered.

"No, you keep him for yourself," she said blankly.

"It's a she," I said. "I want you to take care of her."

I reluctantly put the panda by Grandmom's head and said bye. A week later she came to live with us permanently.

One Saturday evening my parents left Grandmom in charge while they went out for dinner. We watched TV until bedtime and then went upstairs to put on our Dr. Denton's and go to bed.

Without warning, our cat Tippy dashed by with a dead mouse in her mouth. She ran under my bed. I was afraid of mice, but I was more afraid of dead ones. I was sure they would come back to life and crawl over me. I stood screaming in a corner of my room and couldn't move.

"What's the matter, what's the matter?" Grandmom kept repeating as she charged up the stairs.

"Tippy took a mouse under my bed," I cried, flapping my arms. "It's there under my bed."

Grandmom stood at the entrance to my bedroom with her arms crossed over her chest. "It won't hurt you; it's a mouse," she snarled.

"But she has it in her mouth and will let go of it," I wailed.

"You're being a baby," Grandmom said. "Now get into bed before you upset Jeannie and keep her awake."

"No! I'm *not* getting in that bed. Go away! I want my mommy," I screamed.

"Wait until your parents get home and I tell them how bad you are," she threatened. "They'll punish you for giving me trouble. Get into bed *now*," she said angrily.

I didn't care what she said. My fear was overwhelming, and I didn't budge. She stormed across the room and pushed me into bed where I curled up into a ball. After she left the room, Kathleen tried to calm me down. "Sh, it's OK. It's OK," she said calmly.

"I want my mommy," I sobbed. "I don't want Grandmom here. That mouse will come and get me—it will climb all over me and get in my mouth," I explained.

"No, it's OK," she reassured me. "The mouse is dead."

"It doesn't matter if it's dead—it will still get me. Get it out of here," I said. I was shaking, and I moved closer to the headboard.

"I'll take care of it," she said. "Come with me."

"No, I'm not stepping on the floor," I sobbed.

She hurried out of the room, went downstairs to retrieve the broom and dust pan, chased the cat away, and removed the dead mouse. I stayed at the head of the bed where, exhausted, I fell asleep. When I awoke I remembered I had screamed at Grandmom, and expected to be spanked for it. Surprisingly, my parents never mentioned it at all, and I didn't say anything either.

Later in the day, I overheard Mom tell Kathleen that Grandmom shouldn't have added to my fear. Now I liked her less than ever and regretted giving her my panda bear.

Occasionally, however, Mom reminded us to keep Grandmom company and watch TV with her. The door to her suite was always closed. When we knocked she became annoyed. She enjoyed soap operas and watched *Days of Our Lives* and *General Hospital* every day. She also watched wrestling and particularly liked Gorgeous George. She was redeemed only by her rice pudding, her tapioca, and her raisin oatmeal cookies, which she called "rocks." After two months of living with us, even the "rocks" seemed hard.

CHAPTER 10: UNDERCURRENTS

Strange events occurred at our house that I didn't understand until years later. Mink stoles arrived in brown paper bags, which confused me. When Mom shopped at Spears or Weinbergs, two upscale clothing stores in Chester, expensive items were wrapped in white tissue paper and put in white cardboard boxes. But two mink stoles appeared without any wrapping. *A mink stole is special*, I thought. *It seems so ordinary to be in a brown bag with no box and no white tissue paper.*

Dad would phone Leroy and tell him to open the gate to the pasture behind the garage. Leroy opened the gate and waited for the storage vans to arrive. At any given time, the trucks might contain whiskey, appliances, hams, turkeys, or building materials. Whatever was too hot to handle remained on the vans, which were in our pasture hidden among the sixteen acres of woods. Five color TV sets, for example, were unloaded from the van and brought into our back door as "gifts."

Once when I was snooping in my father's cedar closet, I discovered a blue vinyl garment bag. I unzipped it and found piles of dollar bills, each wrapped with a rubber band—one hundred to a pile. Every night Dad counted the bills. When I was old enough to count to a hundred with ease, he asked me to help him. This was a much better way to spend "quality time" with him since it involved no corpses or unpleasant odors.

I loved the earthy aroma of Dad's walk-in cedar closet. I saw his rifles in a glass case with keys attached. Though the rifles intimidated me, I was intrigued by the drawer with no handles beneath the gun case. I watched my mother move the drawer from side to side, which exposed a panel. She tilted the panel toward her revealing a black iron safe. She turned the combination lock to different numbers and opened the safe. Inside were more stacks of dollar bills in rubber bands. There were also blue velvet bags rolled up and bound by gold-braided bands; these bags contained Mom's jewelry.

I tried to memorize the combination when Mom opened the safe. I attempted to open it when my parents were out—twenty-eight left, forty-seven right, three left. I knew the numbers, but the rights and lefts confused me. I couldn't open it.

Dad frequently complained about how little money he made at his practice. He told us there were many poor people he cared for who were unable to pay for his services. He showed me his appointment book, and next to 90 percent of his appointments, it said "N/C," which meant no charge. *Dollar bills? That's all his patients can afford, and Dad still sees them all the time. He must be a saint.* I felt proud to be his daughter.

When I grew up, I learned the truth about the stacks of dollar bills. People came to the kitchen door of the hospital in Chester, said three numbers, and gave money to Big Pearl or other kitchen help. It cost one dollar for three numbers. I had been witnessing the proceeds of a numbers operation! The mink stoles and televisions were payoffs to my father in return for his arrangement of a political endorsement from boss John McClure of the Delaware County Republican Party. Senator McClure had ruled Delaware County for fifty years and was most notorious for the "rum ring trials" of the 1930's.

Though Dad never ran for elective office, both of his positions. coroner's physician and prison physician, were political appointments by Senator McClure. Dad gave the nod for Italians to be endorsed on the Republican ticket.

Dad, known as Dr. Joe, was a formidable figure in the community. As the son of Italian immigrants who came to America in 1890, he did much to foster Italian-American relations. He was the first Italian doctor in Delaware County, and his brother, Anthony, was the first Italian lawyer in the community.

Dad and my uncle were cited as heroes for rescuing many people from the flooding of the Chester River. They pulled people to safety on the banks of the river and attended to their needs. Dad never charged for follow-up treatment for the victims.

Dad was honored four times, once by the Italian government, and given the Star of Solidarity, which recognized how he significantly enhanced Italian-American relationships. Though it wasn't known to me at the time, he paid tuition and expenses for three Italian male students to attend Hahnemann Medical School. Each testimonial banquet was attended by hundreds of people. There were many speeches by state and local politicians citing Dr. Joe's humanitarianism.

In addition to the awards, Dad's status in the community—and eventually nationwide—was enhanced by the expert court testimony he provided in murder cases. Some of the more grotesque homicides that he autopsied, were described in articles in a magazine called *True Detective*. He kept issues of this magazine on his bedside table; the older copies were in the bottom drawer of his dresser.

Dad heard from Mom that I read well, but he never had time to listen to me read from my Scott Foresman reader. Though I was only eight, I read one of the magazine articles about Dad to him aloud to show my advanced reading ability and win his approval. I was astonished to see my father as a famous person.

Years later when I attended high school in Media, the county seat of Delaware County, I would duck out a side door and sometimes walk three blocks to the courthouse if I knew Dad would be testifying in a murder case. Watching Dad place his hand on a Bible and be sworn in impressed me. I heard the silence of the room, and I saw all eyes on him. Judge Guy De Furia acknowledged Dad by nodding to him. The judge declared there was no need to question Dad's credentials. He instructed the attorneys to proceed with relevant questions. When Dad was presented with charts of the human body, he stepped out of the witness box, walked across the marble floor, and used a pointer to emphasize where the bullet had entered and exited the body. Dad was usually swamped by reporters when the trials ended, and he never acknowledged my presence as his daughter. Afterward I walked back to school in empty awe.

While other sources acknowledged Dad's greatness, I was subjected to the dark side of his heart. When I attended, at eight years old, a New Year's Eve party at the Columbus Center, run by the Knights of Columbus, Dad called me to the microphone to tell a dirty joke. The joke went like this. A woman went to the market to buy fresh vegetables. She picked out a cucumber and asked the grocer, "How much?" He told her it was fifty cents. She said, "Fifty cents! You know where you can stick this." He said, "Sorry, madam, but I already have a twenty-five cent banana there." Dad praised me because I performed on stage for the crowd. His infrequent smile was very rewarding. That same night he taught me to dance the box step. I stood on his black polished shoes as he led, and I thought I was the queen - at eight years old no less.

Because I saw hundreds of people honor Dad, I wanted to feel connected to him. I volunteered to set the table at night, and I set my place next to his and across from my mom, which kept the three of us at one end of the table. I set places for my sisters and grandmother at the other end.

Though I was discouraged from expressing my thoughts at dinnertime since children were "to be seen and not heard," I gained the perfect opportunity to listen to adult conversations. Among the topics discussed was hit man Bear, who could pick up a refrigerator in his arms and had broken the legs of an unsuspecting man the night before. I sat quietly and followed the other rules with my left hand resting on the table and my right hand on my lap. My feet were swinging a mile a minute, but there was no rule about what wasn't seen.

Another way to be close to Dad was to sit on his lap or sit next to him in his favorite red lounger while he watched TV. Usually his suspenders were off his shoulders, and his pants were undone. Often he would slide my hand down his pants. Sometimes my hand got slippery and gooey as he guided my hand with his. When he released my hand, he gave me a white linen handkerchief he kept in the side of the chair so I could wipe my hand dry. This was a very quiet, peaceful time, and I regretted getting too big to fit in his chair.

When it was time for bed, my sisters and I performed the daily ritual of kissing my parents goodnight. As I went up the stairs, I always said, "Good night, God bless you, and thank you for all you have done for us today," as instructed by the nuns. But after hearing Mom tell company how nice that was, I decided to substitute the word *us* for *me*.

When I was fourteen and in the ninth grade, I invited my friend Lorraine, to spend the night. At bedtime, I kissed my parents and said my usual thanks. When we were upstairs, Lorraine asked, "You let your father feel you up?" I didn't know what she was talking about. She told me that when I kissed my dad good night he felt my breasts, and that was feeling me up. I shrugged her off and told her,

"That's the way we always say good night. Anyway, my mom said he's allowed to feel any part of me because he's a doctor."

On Monday Lorraine sat in the middle of the school bus, and I sat in the rear. She said, loud enough for everyone to hear, "Julia lets her father feel her up," and she proceeded to tell anyone who was interested what she had observed. I didn't talk to her anymore. I also didn't kiss my parents goodnight anymore or thank them for everything they had done for me.

CHAPTER 11: TAKE NO PRISONERS

As the prison physician at Broadmeadows, the county prison, Dad had to check in daily. Sometimes he would let us ride with him when he drove to the prison on Sunday morning. Once he let me walk with him to individual cells to see "life in prison." On another trip to the prison, the warden presented me with a doll crib painted white and trimmed in pale blue, which the prisoners made in their workshop. Dad frequently drove discharged prisoners to his hospital in Chester. There, the prisoners could catch a train, bus, or the Chester-Bridgeport ferry to their homes.

Sometimes Dad brought inmates to our house to work on the grounds—cutting down trees, replacing spotlights, and building stone walkways. I was with him one Sunday morning when he drove four inmates to our house. As we drove on Conchester Highway, a big, slow dump truck wouldn't let Dad pass. Each time he attempted to pass, the driver swerved in front of him. Growing tired of this game, Dad said to the inmates, "Watch this." He pressed the window button, pulled his pistol out of his shoulder holster, and shot one of the truck's tire. The tire flattened, and the truck pulled over. Dad pulled up behind the truck and told the prisoners to step out of the car. When the trucker saw the four big men, he stepped back into his cab. The inmates were impressed with Dad's accuracy—another reason for me to be proud of him.

"Kathleen, we may be getting a call from the state police." He explained why.

"Joe, you didn't!" she exclaimed. "Not in front of Julia?"

"He was good, Mom," I said. "Just like the Lone Ranger having to shoot the bad guy while he's riding Silver."

Mom was concerned that Dad always carried a gun; so when he came home he would put it under his hat and leave it on the back hall table. One evening Jeannie found the gun and carried it around as if it were a toy. Mom reproached Dad, who responded, "The kids better well leave my gun alone, or I'll break their goddamn arms."

A prisoner named Buck stayed at our house for two weeks while Alice and Leroy were on vacation. One day Jeannie and I—we were eight and nine at the time—were in the basement workshop when Buck entered from the outside door. "What are you doing?" he asked.

"Painting this birdhouse pink," I said. "Jeannie has the red paint, and I have the white, so we're working together."

"Looks OK, but you should have sanded that rough wood."

"The birds won't care."

Jeannie and I continued painting while Buck placed a sheet of plywood on the table. Then he called to us. "Come over here, girls. I have something to show you on the other side of this plywood."

We were curious and walked toward him. He turned the plywood over exposing a poster of a naked woman. He pulled a switchblade from his boot, and using the blade he pointed to her breasts. "Look at her tits," he said. "That's what a woman's tits should be like—big and full." Then he traced the blade to her pubic area. "And look how bushy her hair is. I think a woman's body is a piece of art. Don't you?"

"She's very pretty," I said, grabbing Jeannie by the wrist and running out of the workshop and up the steps. I told Mom, who was more concerned about the knife than the picture and his words.

She confronted Buck later, and he told her he would never hurt us. That episode was never mentioned again.

The following Saturday morning Mom went shopping for groceries. Jeannie and I were to make lunch for Buck. When I entered the kitchen, Jeannie had already made his sandwich. She told me to go to the window that separates the kitchen from the solarium and watch quietly as Buck ate his sandwich. I took my place when she called Buck to come in. He entered the kitchen and said, "What's for lunch?"

"I made you a corned beef sandwich and some lemonade."

Buck bit into the sandwich, shot up from the table, and spit his food into his napkin. "That's not corned beef—that's dog food!" he bellowed. I squelched my giggles. *Yay, Jeannie.* I joined her in the kitchen as his tirade continued.

"I have a friend who works at the University of Pennsylvania, and I'm going to get him to test a sample of this. You'll be in trouble."

"It's the same corned beef Dad had with his eggs at breakfast this morning," I said. "If it was dog food, I'm sure Mom would have heard about it. C'mon, Jeannie, let's go outside and wait for Mom to come home." Once outside we couldn't squelch our giggles. When Mom arrived, I told her what happened, and she grinned.

Buck remained while Alice and Leroy were away. Mom and Dad went on a cruise to the Bahamas. This was their first vacation since our arrival. Grandmom and Mrs. Hyers, a nurse from the hospital, also stayed with us and were responsible for my siblings and me.

Two days after their departure, four state police officers entered our home, in the middle of the night, and searched the premises beginning with the front hall. were in our front hall in the middle of the night. They were shining spotlights behind the statues and in the interior balcony. I climbed out of bed to see what was happening and they commanded me to return to my room and keep the door locked. The next morning I heard what had happened. A store two miles away had been robbed of hundreds of cartons of cigarettes. The owner took the license number, called the police, and gave a description of the robber. The police traced the license number to Dad's jeep; however, the description of the robber didn't match Dad. The state police came to the house looking for the jeep. After talking with Mrs. Hyers, they knew they should look for Buck. The following day they found Buck asleep in the truck in our woods, cartons of cigarettes still in the truck bed. They cuffed him and escorted him back to prison.

One Friday evening around nine o'clock, Dad prepared to close up his office. Scotty, Dad's nurse, called a man thought to be a patient from the waiting room. She told him to go to room four and wait for the doctor. The "patient" pulled a gun on Scotty and demanded all the money in the drawer. Dad was in the hallway; when he heard the demand, he backed into his office, locked the door, and took his gun from the drawer. When he emerged from his office, he instinctively fired down the hall at the robber. Unfortunately one of his patients had leaned out of examining room three to see what was happening and caught the bullet in his back. Dad was able to remove the bullet on the spot. Had it been a few centimeters to the left, the shot would have been fatal. Though the staff was shaken, his patient was understanding. He didn't need to go to the hospital, and Dad provided his aftercare free of charge.

Dad was the victim only once. As he was leaving his office one evening, he fumbled for his keys to unlock his car. A mugger hit him over the head, took his keys, and drove off in Dad's 1962 Cadillac. Dad was dazed. Scotty found him in the parking lot, when she left the office. She called an ambulance and the police. The mugger was apprehended a short time later, and Dad was well enough to have regular office hours the following morning.

CHAPTER 12: A STRING OF FIRSTS

Dad sold Mercy Hospital in 1958 after he had established a practice at Eighth and Kerlin Streets in Chester. Since Mom no longer needed to go to town every day, we attended Saint Thomas the Apostle, the new Catholic elementary school that was two miles from home.

Finally, I have to wear something different! At St. Anthony's we had to wear maroon uniforms with beige blouses, but at St. Thomas we could wear navy-blue uniforms with white blouses. I felt I had a new beginning. They didn't know I was "bad," so I vowed to God and myself, to be extra good. I would be perfect! Mom braided my hair, joined the braids atop my head, and held them together with a barrette. I looked angelic. I kept to myself, completed all my work, and tried to be neat. When I finished my assignments, I folded my hands, put them on top of my desk, and sat up straight waiting for the next instruction. One day while we were saying the rosary after lunch, Sister Catherine Angela kept looking at me, but she said nothing. I was sure she saw a halo around me. At that moment I realized I would be a saint when I died. I was so pious.

Another day some of the students solved math problems at the blackboard. We were each to work three long division problems involving decimals. I returned to my seat feeling confident as I watched Sister mark many of the other students wrong. I gloated. *It's so nice to be away from Saint Anthony's where I am the smartest in the class.* To my chagrin, Sister Catherine put a big *X* over my first problem; she paused and put a big *X* over my second; she paused again and put a darker *X* over the third. All eyes were on me, as I felt my cheeks flush. I lowered my head and cried. My persona was shattered—I made mistakes I had tried so hard not to make. I cried as much for erring as I did knowing I would be denied sainthood when I died. I wasn't perfect, and I knew Sister Catherine wouldn't see my halo again.

In fifth grade I fell in love with a classmate, Billy. His birthday party was the first I ever attended. We had fun singing "Witch Doctor" and feasting on hot dogs, chips, and birthday cake. We played spin the bottle and post office, both kissing games. The following Monday, Billy gave me a silver "going steady" ring. I placed it on my ring finger and showed everyone. No other girl was going steady—this was groovy. Two days later my finger turned green. Noticing the discoloration, Dad said, "Julia, take that ring off. It's not healthy."

"But this ring is special," I answered. "Billy gave it to me."

"It's not special—he got it from a gum machine, and it's turning your finger green."

"He didn't get it from a gum machine. He got it from the Booth Corner's Farmer Market, and it cost a dollar twenty-five."

"Take it off and give it back to him."

"Use soap," Mom suggested. I twisted the ring, but it didn't budge, and my finger began to swell. I went to the bathroom, turned on the water, and slid the bar of Ivory up and down my finger. The ring still didn't move. It was clear to Mom and Dad that intervention was needed. Dad called Leroy from the basement and told him to bring the wire cutters. Tears streamed down my cheeks, as Leroy cut the ring without cutting me. *How would I tell Billy?* I wondered. *He paid money for the ring, and he'll think I don't want to go with him, I thought. I'll tell him the ring came off while I was washing the dishes. I put it on the window sill and forgot about it. Later, when I went to retrieve the ring, it wasn't there. Rosie probably took it.* But the next morning Rosie beat me to the punch. She told everyone in the class that my ring had to be cut off and that Dad said it probably came from a gum machine. Billy hung his head and didn't speak to me.

So I turned my attention to John, whom every girl liked. He had blond hair and blue eyes, and he was the smartest in the class. I sent him a note across the aisle, which read, "I want to marry you and live in a trailer with a white picket fence and have twenty-four kids." He responded, "The milk bill will be too high." Our steady relationship was short lived.

Whenever we rode to the hospital with Mom, she would drive under a railroad bridge where we sometimes saw the "silver train," which took people to faraway places. Mom told Jeannie and me it was special because passengers could eat and sleep on it. She promised that someday we'd get to ride it. That summer of my fifth-grade year, Mom kept her promise. Aunt Mary and Uncle Emmett invited Jeannie and me to spend two weeks with them. Jeannie and

I were to travel by train, that is, the silver train. We were to board the train in Philadelphia and take it to Jacksonville, Florida, where Aunt Mary and Uncle Emmett would meet us and drive us to their house in Satsuma, Florida.

We were two children traveling alone for twenty-three hours. Since I was the oldest, my responsibility was to take care of Jeannie. A social worker from the Children's Aid Society instructed me on travel safety. "You have to be alert—there are men out there just watching for children traveling alone. Don't talk with anyone, and see that your sister doesn't either."

Dad pinned money on the inside of my t-shirt and my underpants. "Just in case you're robbed, you'll have money, but don't let anyone know. The train will stop at different places along the way, but stay in your seats and don't get off."

We boarded the train, and Jeannie sat in the window seat. Nothing exciting happened. I realized that what had impressed me when I saw the train over the bridge was how fast it went and how pretty the silver looked. But once inside the train, I saw none of that—I only saw rows and rows of seats. Some of the countryside would have been pretty, but I had to stretch over Jeannie to look, and it passed by quickly.

A train steward escorted us to the dining car, and I—feeling very grown up—paid for the meal without using my underwear money. When either of us needed to use the bathroom, both of us went. The train made several stops, but I remembered Dad telling us to stay in our seats. Jeannie slept most of the way, but I tried to stay awake—after all I was to be on the lookout for "men who were out there just looking for children traveling alone."

Jeannie was asleep, and it was dark outside. The passengers around me slept, and a couple of them snored. From out of nowhere, two men entered our car—one was thin, and he was chasing a fat man. Both of them had dark skin. The thin man yelled, "Stop, stop. I'll kill you—I'll kill you." And with that the fat man lost his balance and ended up in my lap. The other man had a gun pointed at him. *These must be the men who are looking for children traveling alone,* I thought. *The Children's Aide Society lady wasn't just trying to scare me. What should I do now?*

A woman seated across the aisle awoke startled. She bellowed, "What the hell's going on here?" The man in my lap jumped up, and the chase continued down the aisle. I felt for my underwear money, and to my relief the pins were secure.

I shook Jeannie's shoulder. "Wake up, wake up. These two men were—"

She stopped me mid-sentence and groggily said, "Julia, will you shut up and go to sleep?" *Jeannie won't listen, and I'm not to talk to anyone else.* I put my hat over my face while silent tears of frustration rolled down my cheeks.

When we arrived in Florida, Aunt Mary and Uncle Emmett greeted us with smiles. Jeannie looked refreshed, but I had circles under my eyes. Although I was tired, I told them about the excitement on the train. They smiled at each other as if they thought I had made up the story. My credibility improved later in the day, when two FBI agents arrived at their home to question me about the incident on the train. After questioning me the FBI said my description of the two men was consistent with the adults they interviewed. They told my aunt and uncle the two men had boarded in Georgia.

When the train crossed state lines, the FBI became involved. The two men jumped from the train somewhere in Florida and were on the run. Aunt Mary and Uncle Emmett phoned Mom and Dad and told them what happened. Mom and Dad arranged for us to fly home two weeks later. I enjoyed air travel much more than riding the rails.

When we arrived home, the school year was approaching. In sixth grade I thought I was special because another classmate, Kathleen, and I were selected to be the leaders of the May procession. We were the same size, and we would lead the first graders followed by the rest of the students. We bought identical white dresses and were ready to go. Two days before the procession, however, we were involved in throwing a banana peel around the classroom during lunch. When Sister Claire Elizabeth walked in on this scene, Kathy and I were sent to Mother Mary Aloysius's office where we were punished. We were not allowed to lead the procession, and we were reduced to bringing up the rear. This demotion was easier to take with another person involved. We chitchatted and smiled with each other since no one could see us anyhow.

A year later I was in seventh grade. Cleaning the nun's convent was an exclusive privilege of seventh - and eighth-graders on Friday afternoons. One Friday while I vacuumed and dusted Mother Aloysius's bedroom, Satan tapped my shoulder, and I opened one of her dresser drawers. Inside there were neatly folded brassieres and underwear. I unfolded one of the mammoth brassieres and was surprised. *I wear a 32-AA. These must at least be 50-ZZ.* I had no idea nuns wore anything except their habits and starched bibs. I discovered a well-hidden fact, and I was eager to share it with the other girls. I put Mother Mary's bra over my clothes and skipped down the hall chanting, "Look-ie what I found. Look-ie what I found." The other girls didn't share my joy, nor did Sister Claire Elizabeth who entered the front door as I skipped to the entrance.

"Julia," she reprimanded, "that's sacrilegious! Take that off right now, and go back to the classroom." That was the last time I was permitted to clean.

That same year, 1960, when John F. Kennedy and Richard Nixon ran for the presidency, I noticed that Dad was interested in the outcome of the election. Although I was only twelve, I followed the campaigns on TV with him. On election day, Dad voted at our local fire hall in Boothwyn but worked at the polling site in Chester. I observed the process with him throughout the day and I was excited.

That night we watched TV and waited for the returns. Kennedy was declared the winner. "Well, he won the election," Dad said. "We better prepare for four years of war."

"Why do you say that?" I asked.

"He's the first Catholic president, and he's a Democrat. In the past whenever Democrats were elected, there was a war."

The following day everyone at school seemed happy except me; I was a Nixon supporter. Sister Claire exclaimed, "This is a wonderful time we live in when a Catholic could win a national election!" She used the election as a civics lesson and asked, "Why is it good to vote?" She called on me.

"It is good to vote, Sister, because you get paid."

"Get paid? Nobody gets paid for voting."

"Yes they do," I responded. "Yesterday I went with Dad to the polls, and I saw him give a new dollar bill to each person who said they'd vote Republican. Later when they came to vote again, they got another dollar bill."

I was proud that I was the only kid in the class to answer Sister's question. I couldn't wait until dinner to tell Dad and Mom. I waited for the perfect moment. I wanted it to be nice and quiet for my big contribution to the otherwise adult conversation. When I told them Sister's question and my answer, they looked at each other in silence, rolled their eyes, and looked up toward the ceiling. Dad quickly changed the subject and talked about an operation he had performed. This was not the reaction I expected.

The next year Sister Claire Elizabeth gave us the sex talk, which fell somewhat short of a lesson in anatomy. The only thing she said was, "And remember, boys and girls, whatever you do in the marriage state is not a sin." Kids in the class looked at each other and smiled. *Being married lets you do anything you want,* I thought. *That means if I get married, I can lie, cheat, rob, beat someone up, or even kill, and I will have no black marks on my soul. I wanted to get married even more. And I wondered if Blair was interested.*

One Monday morning a classmate, Philomena, told three of us girls she had something to share when we had our lavatory break. From her hushed tone, we expected something juicy. Once in the bathroom, she called us over to the end stall. "I started working at a pharmacy over the weekend," she gushed. "And I found out men have periods like women do, and they have to wear something like a pad. This guy came into the store and asked to talk with the pharmacist. They didn't know I was listening, but I overheard the customer ask for 'rectarines,' and from what I heard, it's a pad men have to put up their bottoms."

"No, that can't be true," I said. "Only girls have periods, and if you talk to a boy about your period, that's how you get pregnant. I know because my older sister told me that. We better stop talking about this now." Enlightened, we returned to class and gave the boys a knowing smile. Years later I discovered that "rectarines" were suppositories.

Over the years I had established a strong bond with Mom. I had always been protective of her feelings. One year nobody remembered her birthday except for me. I told her that my gift of the white beaded purse was from Dad and that he had asked me to give it to her. She was perceptive. She knew the truth and was hurt. She cried, and I cried with her.

One day she was yelling at Rosie, Jeannie, and me about our failure to keep our rooms neat. When we all ignored her, she dumped our clothes from our drawers onto the floor and began raging. "I knew it," she said. "You can't make a silk purse out of a sow's ear. Your parents were white trash, and you will be too. You would have still been sitting your ass in the orphanage if we hadn't taken you." I was surprised and insulted.

"No!" I said at the top of my lungs. "God would have taken us, and God didn't even want you to have children. He knew you wouldn't be a good mother. You had to go and take someone else's children." Mom grabbed me by my Ben Casey shirt, tore off the buttons, left the room, and slammed the door behind her. I had no idea where the acid words and loud voices of the two of us came from. She left me with a lot to think about. For one thing, I didn't know what a sow was and wouldn't until years later. Also, that was the first time I heard the term "white trash," and I just guessed of the meaning. Rosie explained that it didn't mean white-lined, loose-leaf paper scrunched up and put in the wastebasket. I didn't believe my mother. She didn't know anything about my parents, and she probably just said that to make herself feel better. I resolved to one day find out the truth someday and prove her wrong. I intended to tell Dad on her, but Rosie said he'd believe her and not me. I found large safety pins and pinned my shirt at each buttonhole. I thought since he was a doctor, he'd ask me about my Ben Casey shirt and what had happened, but he didn't. I never apologized to Mom; nor was I asked to.

At some point our relationship was restored, and we made our peace. Since the hospital had been sold, Dad suggested that Mom volunteer for the women's auxiliary at Crozier Hospital. On Friday nights she wheeled the gift cart for patients and visitors to purchase items such as magazines, candy bars, pens, and stationery. This was the highlight of my early teen years. While my sisters went to a dance at the local fire hall, I helped Mom at the hospital. I cherished these times. I was with her and helping others at the same time. We usually left the hospital around ten o'clock when Dad closed his office. We would meet him at Linton's restaurant, where I always ordered a strawberry sundae with strawberry ice cream topped with whipped cream and three cherries. This made both of them smile because it was so late at night. Dad liked it when I ate like this. I loved the time that just belonged to the three of us.

One Friday night Mom thought it was time for me attend a dance with my sisters. I felt awkward. I had been told I had no sense of rhythm. The words of "Let the Little Girl Dance" by Billy Bland resounded in my head:

> She's been a little wallflower on the shelf,
> Standing by herself.
> Never had the nerve to take a chance,
> So let the little girl dance.
> Let the little girl through,
> She wants to dance with you.
> She wants to give it a try,
> So let the little girl by.

No one asked me to dance, and I never attended a dance again.

CHAPTER 13: READY OR NOT

After eighth grade my sisters and I were allowed to choose whether we would attend a Catholic high school or switch to public. Without hesitation we all chose public. Since there was no senior high school where we lived, I attended Garnet Valley for the ninth grade, then Media High School until I graduated.

Year after year in elementary school, the nuns criticized the public schools to the class The public schools don't teach religion. Public school kids are wild. Anyone can get by in public school. There is no discipline. Those kids are allowed to do whatever they want. I was particularly intrigued by the last comment. *Yes! I can do anything I want. This sounds like the "married state" Sister described. This means I can talk back, I won't get homework, I won't have to stand up to answer questions, and—since there is no discipline—there won't be any hitting kids with yardsticks. I'll be able to chew gum and eat candy whenever I want. I'm ready!*

Since kindergarten I'd had to wear a uniform, and now I was able to dress like regular kids. Instead of the boys sitting on one side of the room and the girls on the other, we were integrated, which I liked. There were more boys ripe for the picking!

I got in trouble early in the year for talking back to Mr. Busby, who was my homeroom teacher as well as my science teacher. He was my first male instructor—and oh so cute.

Because science was difficult for me, I found other ways to occupy class time. One day I brought a Milky Way to class, unwrapped it carefully, popped a large piece in my mouth, and chewed away. I felt good that I had succeeded in being sneaky until Mr. Busby looked at me.

"Are you chewing gum?" he suddenly asked. I shook my head. "You're chewing on something," he said. "Give it to me." He walked down the aisle toward my desk. I slid out on the other side of the desk and moved toward the back of the room. As he came toward the back, I crossed to another row and advanced to the front of the room, still chewing and swallowing my Milky Way. *If I can only keep moving, I'll have this finished. He's so cute I can't spit this out in his hand*. But seeing my pattern, he took long strides to the front of the room and cornered me at the blackboard. The class was laughing which didn't shame me; if anything, the teacher looked foolish. "OK, Julia," he said as his cupped his hand in front of me. "Spit the rest of it out." I expelled the rest of it into his hand. "Oooh, gross," the class said in unison. Mr. Busby wiped his hand with a tissue. He accompanied me to the principal's office, where I was assigned my first detention.

Another time in science class, I brought *The Bramblebush*, a paperback book from home that Mom had discarded. I'd overheard Mom describing the story to her friend, and she said it had a lot of sex in it, like the book *Peyton Place. That sounds interesting. I'll bring it to school and share it with my friends. First I'll pick out the good parts and underline them.*

I went to school and told my girlfriend Suzanne of my find. I informed her that when I got to a good part, I would pass it across the aisle when Mr. Busby's back was turned. As planned, I opened my science textbook, placed it between my lap and the desk, and positioned *The Bramblebush* inside the book. I read and underlined.

One part describes rabbits "doing it." I looked across the aisle at Suzanne and waited for the opportunity. But in passing the book, I dropped it to the floor. When Mr. Busby picked it up, I was embarrassed. I wished I hadn't underlined the juicy parts. So it was another walk to the office, another detention, and—this time—a phone call to Mom, who was highly embarrassed.

Later in the year, I wrote a note to Suzanne and passed it across the aisle. It read, "Hi, Suzanne. Do you think Mr. Busby is cute? I do. He's the cutest teacher in the whole school. Mr. Cunningham looks nerdy. Mr. Moser looks like a monkey. But when Mr. Busby smiles, he's so dreamy. I would like to have him for my boyfriend. I wonder if he and his wife 'do it.' Write back." Suzanne answered and passed the note back, but Mr. Busby turned around at that exact moment. I quickly raised the lid of my desk to shield me, and I put the note in my mouth. He thought I had thrown it in my desk. "Stand up," he said. He sat at my desk and shuffled through my books and papers, which gave me time to exit the class, go to the girl's room, and flush the note. Mr. Busby met me at the doorway of the lavatory and escorted me to the office, where Mr. Rumford, the assistant principal (who was the second cutest teacher), assigned me a third detention and called Mom.

Algebra was another difficult subject, and Mr. Moser, the teacher, didn't make it any easier. I didn't understand what letters had to do with numbers. I thought maybe it was a code, *a* stood for one, *b* stood for two, and so forth. But that wasn't correct. *A* plus *b* must obviously be *c*. "Where do they come up with *ab* as the answer?" I asked aloud. Most of the class had been exposed to pre-algebra, but my experience was limited to addition, subtraction, multiplication, division, fractions, decimals, and percentages. Math had always been one of my strengths, and I usually attained grades between 90 and 100 percent.

The class was divided into two sections, A and B. A was for the smart ones; B included me and two others. Once again I was bored. Kelsey sat in front of me and always wore skintight short dresses. I took a thumbtack off Mr. Moser's desk and had it ready. I placed it on Kelsey's seat right before class began. I was in a prime position to see her reaction. "Aayee!" she screamed as she shot straight up in the air. *Wow, that was more than I expected*. Mr. Moser accompanied me to the office and told Mr. Rumford he would not have me in class anymore.

Oh well, what's one more detention? And I would love it if I didn't have to take algebra. But Mr. Rumford had other ideas. "Take a seat," he yelled. "I'll deal with you after speaking with Principal Ramsay." I sat there in thought: *Mrs. Ramsay and her husband have been to my house twice for dinner. Mr. Rumford doesn't know they are friends of the family. Mrs. Ramsay will tell him to send me back to class and give me another chance.*

He called me into Mrs. Ramsay's office as she was leaving. He stood straight with both hands behind his back. "You have had three detentions for three different offenses," he lectured. "And now you have caused pain to another student." He exposed the paddle behind him, emphasizing the holes for stinging. "Bend over," he said.

"No," I said without emotion while sitting on the couch. "You can't make me."

"What did you say?"

"No, I'm not going to, and you can't make me," I repeated. "I'll just sit here until school is over and you've left. I'll call Leroy to come and pick me up."

I must have given him an idea. He backed away to the desk and picked up the phone receiver. “What is your phone number?” he asked. I knew where this was going.

“Globe nine two five four eight,” I said, hoping the number would ring and no one would answer.

“Hello. I’m Mr. Rumford from Garnet Valley school” He paused. “Oh, sorry, I must have a wrong number.” I looked to my right at the bookcases. “I guess I’ll have to look up your number since you must not know it,” he said sarcastically.

He left the office momentarily. *I can’t bend over. I wore two different silk stockings, and my one garter is longer than the other—he’s sure to notice. He’ll probably tell Mr. Busby about it, and Mr. Busby will never want to go with me.* He returned to the office carrying a large index card.

“Well, it was almost right,” he said before dialing GL-925.

“OK,” I interrupted, “I’ll bend over.” He replaced the receiver on its cradle. And with my uneven stockings and garter exposed, he hauled off and gave me a swat. I stood up straight, looked at him, and said, “Is that all?”

"Bend over again," he said. *Damn, I shouldn't have said that.* He put more force into the second swat. He administered an additional mental swat as he led me to the phone and told me to call Mom. He watched closely as I dialed. I explained the incident to Mom, who said that we would discuss it later. When I arrived home that day I found out that Mrs. Ramsay and Mom had talked before the paddling, and that Mom had already approved the action. The ordeal had a bright side; it earned me the distinction of having been the first girl paddled in the history of Garnet Valley Junior High. I thought I was tough, and the boys began to notice me.

Later in the year, I wrote possible answers to a science test on the palm of my hand. But later in the class, I made the mistake of raising my hand. The next punishment was a one day suspension.

"No," I told the assistant principal, " you can't do that. Dad just had a heart attack. My parents told me not to tell anyone. This suspension would probably cause another attack." Mr. Rumford ignored me. "You don't even care if my father has a heart attack," I yelled. "You'll be responsible for his death." Despite my pleas, I was suspended, and required to inform my parents of this action.

Before I could return, they had to sign the discipline paper. I was afraid to tell my parents, knowing they would probably disown me and tell me I was a disgrace to the family name.

How would I tell them? I have no idea what Dad will do. Once, when Mom told him my sisters and I had misbehaved, he said, "Why didn't you just throw them over the goddamn balcony?" And I had no doubt he would do that. I know—I'll hurt myself. Since Dad's a doctor, he'll have sympathy for me and will be more concerned about my injury.

I decided to break my leg. I climbed the ladder to the hayloft, walked back to the far wall, and took a running leap to the ground. I landed on both feet and nothing broke, twisted, or sprained. I landed with a thud. *All I've done is make me even shorter, and now I still have to tell them.* I was disappointed and thought about another jump, but I didn't want to be shorter.

When I told my parents, they already knew and said they weren't going to do anything more since I had been punished at school. I was angry because I had tried to hurt myself when it wasn't necessary to waste my energy. During that year I realized the nuns had lied to me in elementary school—public school wasn't easy, and they had discipline. I thoroughly understood this, and the next fall I intended to reform.

At the beginning of the year, I was in the C section for average kids but was moved to the B section after I made the honor roll in the first six weeks. I was elected secretary of the class, and my parents weren't called about my behavior. I did, however, occasionally play hooky and talk out of turn.

I once agreed to climb into a round, dark-green metal trash can and let two of my friends roll me down a flight of steps. *This sounds like fun*. When I came to a stop and pushed the lid off the can, I looked up and saw the principal, Mr. Barrall. He glared at me.

"Your parents," he said, "would be very disappointed in you."

"Then by all means," I answered, "don't tell them." He actually smiled at me and never told.

That same year I discovered boys in a more serious way. I was going steady. *Now I fit in with some of the girls, and I'm better than some who don't have a boyfriend.*

I had kissed and hugged a few boys since I was ten years old, but this year I fell in love with Mike. He was cute with his short brown hair and his black horn-rimmed glasses. We used to find empty classrooms after school and make out.

One day after school, I purposely missed my bus so I would have to take the sports bus two hours later. Mike lived within a few blocks and urged me to walk him home. His parents were working, and his brother wasn't around; so we went up to his room, kissed, and rubbed our bodies against each other. Next thing I knew I was lying on the bed with my dress up and my underwear off; I was in a trance. That was called "making love." The next day Scott, a classmate, informed me that Mike told him I didn't move during sex. If I wanted, he said, he would teach me how girls are suppose to act.

The next Saturday Scott came to my house. We rode my horse through the woods until we came to a deserted spot where he could instruct me properly. We dismounted and made love "like boys expect." Now I understood what all the fuss was about!

On Monday after school, Scott told Mike about our tryst. Mike broke up with me, and I was totally devastated. Though my classmates knew and didn't make fun of me, I was very ashamed of this rejection. I didn't want anyone in my family to know.

Soon after that our class went on a field trip to Hershey Park. Sometime during the day, Scott and I made our way back to the bus to make out. I came home with a big hickey (or, as Mom irreverently called it, a "suck mark") on my neck. I tried to hide it, but it was above my collar line.

"Mom," I exclaimed as I entered the house. "You won't believe what happened to me. I was walking along with Ellen, minding my own business, when I heard someone call my name. I looked to my left, and wham! Just like that, the right side of my neck hit the corner of a Ferris wheel seat."

Alarmed, she said, "Let me see. That looks like a suck mark."

"What is a suck mark?"

"It's a bruise from someone sucking on your neck."

"Mom, I would know if someone was sucking on my neck. How can you think such a thing?" I asked. "It's like you don't trust me, and I've never given you any reason not to."

"Well," she said, "you *are* boy crazy."

I put my hands on my hips and looked her straight in the eyes. "Well, that didn't happen. Remember, Mom, we went as a group." With a sigh, she said, "Go to bed. It's been a long day."

"OK, Mom, I will. Good night. Love you."

Thinking it over, I decided to tell her the "truth." The next day I confessed it was Mike who gave me the suck mark. Of course Mom said I could never date him again. This gave me the perfect out. I didn't have to let my family know I had been rejected. I cried for young love lost. My mood was erratic. I repeatedly banged my head against the wood-paneled wall yelling, "Nobody loves me." There wasn't a soul in the house who told me otherwise.

Ever since age ten, I had migraine headaches. They became more intense and frequent. Mom didn't understand why I, of all the kids, got headaches since she saw me as calm and never bothered by anything. Dad told me to take Darvon Compound, which never helped my headaches and upset my stomach.

One evening I thought, *if one Darvon doesn't help me, maybe I'm just not taking enough.* So I took six. That night I went with my friend Mandy to visit a classmate at the hospital. I told Mandy what I had done and how everything was feeling strange to me—like things were floating and slowing me down. She phoned Mom and told her. Then Mandy drove me home, and Mom phoned Dad, who told her to keep me awake with coffee. When he arrived home he bounded through the door, his face red.

"How can you be so goddamn stupid?" he yelled.

"You call yourself a doctor," I screamed, taking the offensive," you can't even take care of my headaches. You take care of everybody else, but you don't take care of your family." This said, I hurriedly found my way to my room and locked the door. Nothing more was ever said.

The next year I fell in love with Jack. He was in the honors section, played first trumpet, dressed nicely, had a lean build, and had an innocent look about him with his blond hair and blue eyes. He came from an intelligent, philosophical, soft-spoken family. Though normally serious, he could be given to banter if I started it. That year he let his hair grow long. Jack got in a little trouble here and there; he joined a group of five students teachers referred to as "the unholy five." Mr. Jenkins, who taught college-bound

English, was sure that I had influenced Jack so negatively. Jack asked me to go steady with him on November 9, 1963, and I said, "Yeah, OK." We stayed together and dated only each other throughout high school.

In my junior year, we had a talent show. Seven of my girlfriends and I decided to perform the song, "*On the Good Ship Lollipop,*" and from there we would shed some of our little girl clothing down to our black body suits and leotards to "*The Stripper.*" The night of the performance, while I was in the gym putting on my costume, someone came in and told me my parents were in the audience. Mom and Dad had never come to any school functions. I had trouble breathing; I felt like I was floating in water and suddenly sucked under in a whirlpool. My heart pounded. I sat under a piano with my knees crossed to my chest and my arms wrapped securely around them; again I felt the invisible shield. One of my classmates told a teacher who was working backstage. He talked gently to me and encouraged me to take some deep breaths. I came around, got dressed, went on stage, and performed. Our act was well received and was recognized as the most creative number.

On the way home, the only thing Dad said was that a teacher told him what happened with me. Dad told me not to act that way again or people would think I was "goddamn crazy." He never once said anything about the performance. I didn't tell him about the numerous other times when I was alone and felt the symptoms. But no one helped me get through those times. He was a medical doctor and could have told me I was having panic attacks.

Early in my senior year, several of my classmates applied to college. Some of the girls were engaged and looked forward to marriage right out of school. Jack and I both applied to Pennsylvania State University. He had combined College Board scores of over 1400, while I had only 545 in verbal and 339 in math. Included in the application was a section on health; I had checked off "frequent headaches" and added "migraines." Dad saw it and said, "Why did you put that down?" dad asked as he read the application. "They're not going to want you. They'll think you're not right."

"I'm only being honest," I said. I mailed my application. Jack and everyone else who applied to Penn State had been notified of the institution's decision, not, but I heard nothing. *Now,* I figured, *Dad was correct—they'll think you're not right. And that's why I didn't hear anything.*

Mrs. ElizabethTaylor, the dean, called me to the guidance office. "When and where did you send your application?" she asked. "You should have heard one way or another."

"In October," I said. "I sent it to Mr. Willard Hall at Penn State."

"Mr. Willard Hall?" she asked with a smile. "Willard Hall is the name of the administrative office. It's a building, not a person." I had seen the name on the enclosed envelope, and I thought: *I don't know him and should not be addressing him by his first name. I'll be respectful and add "Mr."* I submitted another application. This time I did not check "frequent headaches."

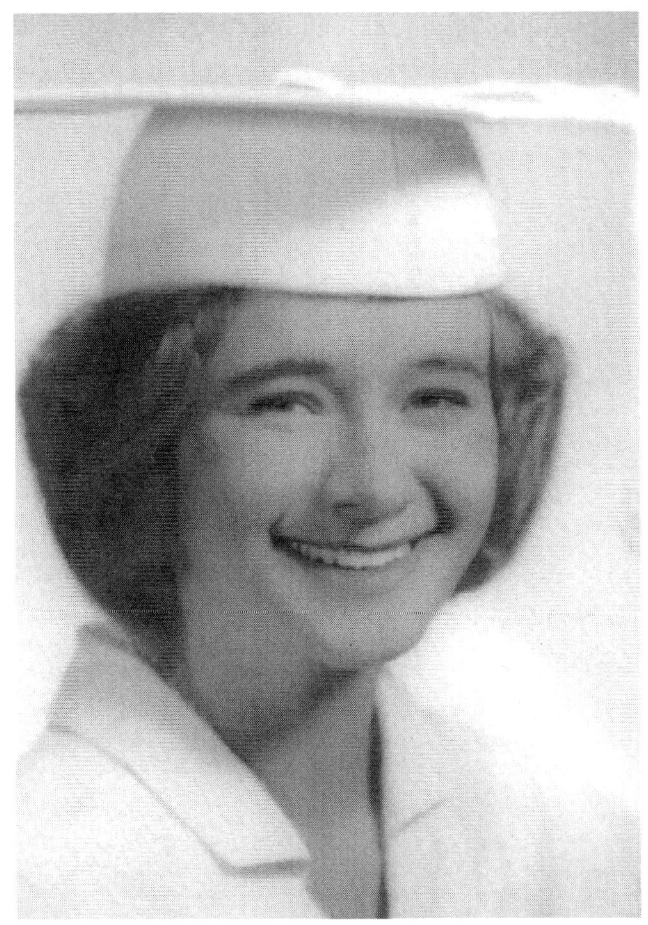

Yes ! I made it.

CHAPTER 14: ON MY OWN

I was accepted to Penn State, but it was so late in the year that the main campus assignments were taken. I was assigned to the Mont Alto commonwealth campus. Mont Alto is located in Franklin County, a rural area in central Pennsylvania where the closest town was fourteen miles away. Mont Alto campus had been a forestry school housing only males. But it became coeducational in 1965. While the guys majored in surveying and forestry, the gals were mostly liberal arts majors.

My roommate's name was Frankie, short for Francine. We were assigned to a suite with three rooms located at the end of the hall. Two other girls, Sissy and Helena, shared the quarters. Sissy had a boyfriend at home, while Helena immediately fell in love with Larry. Frankie eventually fell in love with another student, Jeremy. I was still going with Jack, who was at the main campus. We corresponded—I wrote to him, at least.

Our housemother was an elderly woman whose apartment was in the middle of the dormitory. Every Saturday morning she would drive to town; if you had behaved that week, you could accompany her. In an effort to win this privilege, I would go to her suite to socialize. Meanwhile, Frankie made soup on a hot plate, which was against the rules. Frankie's father owned a hardware store, so we were well equipped.

Many of the girls in the dormitory were from Philadelphia, and they were used to public transportation. They were homesick and often irritable. They thought all the guys on campus were hicks, and treated them in a condescending manner. They frequently phoned their families to come and take them home. I wasn't homesick; but to pass the time I played pinochle—cut throat, airplane, or double-deck—night and day. I missed classes over pinochle and didn't study because of pinochle.

Frankie's boyfriend, Jerry, lived off campus in a cabin in the woods roughly a half mile away where I commenced my career in pinochle. Our room had a distinct feature: our window used to be a door, and it had steps leading to the outside. We had a midnight curfew, but we'd put our pillows under the covers to make it look as if there were bodies in beds. Then we would sneak out to play pinochle at Jerry's cabin and return when we were ready. Before we went, I would usually visit the housemother to chat; and after thirty minutes I would yawn and announce my intention to retire. As a result she never checked our room.

Some of the girls from Philadelphia didn't care for Frankie, and they told the dean she was sneaking out at night. The dean made a new rule: the next person caught out after curfew would go home on the next train and would not be able to return until his or her parents met with him. Frankie and I continued our pinochle sessions at Jerry's. One night when we returned through our window, the housemother was sitting on my bed waiting for us with drooping eyelids and hands folded in her lap. The dean didn't send us home on a train; instead we were to call our parents and tell them they had to come to campus and meet with him. When I phoned Mom and told her she had to talk to the dean, she was certain I was either pregnant or flunking. I was appalled she should think either.

Mom had her friend Hannah drive her to campus, which seemed strange since she liked to drive. She talked with the dean and was told that I had broken curfew. She thought the matter unimportant as I did and was relieved to know I wasn't pregnant or flunking out. After our parents met with the dean, Frankie said, "You know if you put glue in a door lock, no one will be able to unlock the door." She gave me a small bottle of Elmer's, and that evening after dinner none of the girls from Philadelphia could open the doors to their rooms.

When my sister Kathleen drove to the campus to bring me home for Thanksgiving break, she told me matter-of-factly, with eyes glued to the road, "Mom is sick in bed. She had a breast removed last week. When you see her, don't let on that you know. Just act natural." When I saw Mom looking so fragile, I smiled and made small talk about unbroken curfews, grades, and friends. I returned to school without her or Dad telling me about her illness.

My grades were rotten in the first semester. I earned an F in Spanish, a D in theatre, a D in music, and a B in political science. When I returned from semester break, I took a part-time job in the library, mostly to earn money but also to stay out of trouble.

Some evenings no students used the library, and I was bored. I shelved books and straightened the magazine racks, but it was dull. I became fascinated with the electric eraser in the library. I experimented with it, rubbing the eyes off people pictured on the cover of *Time* and other magazines. Word circulated that the school psychologist was looking for whoever was erasing eyes and had declared that person sick. Though I saw nothing wrong with it, I stopped before I was caught.

The second semester I earned all Cs; in the third term, all B's. I studied hard during the third term, especially the nights before finals when I would stay up half the night studying. One such night I walked to the bathroom, in the basement of the building; in returning, I noticed the fire alarm. It read, "IN CASE OF FIRE BREAK GLASS." *How would breaking the glass help put out a fire?* I impulsively pulled the fire alarm. I never anticipated the commotion it would cause. The dorm was evacuated at three in the morning. Screaming fire trucks raced to the scene, but it was declared a false alarm. The dean said he would discover who pulled the alarm and press charges. I told no one. The mystery remained.

In the spring of my freshman year, I visited Penn State's main campus to spend the weekend with Jack at his dormitory, which was constructed of gray stone covered with ivy, in the collegiate gothic style. His roommate was away. Coeds, of course, were not permitted to stay in the men's dorms; so Jack gave me a baseball cap and large jacket as a disguise. Although we slept together, Jack seemed distant. He was quiet and seemed absorbed in his own thoughts. I realized we were growing apart. We didn't see each again until June, when we went home for the summer.

By then Mom's secret was out. The anti-cancer drug Cytoxin and chemotherapy caused her hair to fall out and her skin to flake. While never more than 130 pounds, her weight had dropped to one hundred. I held back the tears since I was told not to mention her condition. We said nothing about feelings, but I missed her usual vigor. I resolved to take care of her. Mom was too weak to walk upstairs; so Dad put a hospital bed in our solarium, which became her bedroom. Dad continued to sleep in their bedroom.

In addition to my mother's health, I had my own concerns. I hadn't had my period since May. I told my sister Mary, an obstetrician and pediatrician.

"Julia, for Christ's sake!" she yelled. "Why the hell weren't you on the pill?"

"Why would I want to prevent myself from getting pregnant?" I asked, surprised by her reaction. "If God wants me to have a baby, why would I use a pill to prevent it? The pill seems against nature." Although Mary was upset, I wasn't. Clearly, the lack of a proper course in sex education had led to my naiveté. I told Jack, but he didn't share my excitement.

"Did you sleep with anyone at school during the year?" he asked.

"No, I didn't," I said, insulted. "How can you even suggest such a thing when you and I have been going steady for three years?" We discussed the situation and decided to tell his father first since he had a calm nature. Jack's dad shook his head. "What are you kids going to do?" he asked.

"What do you mean?" I asked. "There is only one thing to do. We'll get married, of course. I won't put the baby up for adoption."

I paused. "I have friends who got pregnant, and they went to Elkton, Maryland, to get married. We need to have an adult present to sign the consent." His dad agreed to sign on the condition that we tell my family and seek their advice. He volunteered to break the news to Jack's mom.

Since Mom was sick, I suggested we only tell Dad. We visited him in his office on a Friday evening thinking he wouldn't be as upset if his patients were within earshot. Mrs. Scott, his nurse, told us to wait in his private office. The large mahogany desk, leather chairs, sofa, and mahogany-paneled wall were daunting. Behind his desk, oil paintings of his family graced the entire wall. Mom's portrait was in the center. Mary and Helen, his daughters from his first marriage, were on either side of Mom. Kathleen and Rosie were next to them, and Jeannie and I were at the ends. I had been in his office many times before but had never paid attention to these details.

Sitting in the wingback chairs facing his desk, I felt dwarfed. Dad entered and sat in his chair behind the desk. He opened the top drawer, pulled a pistol from the holster beneath his jacket, and placed it in the drawer. He relit a cigar, which was sitting in the glass ashtray.

"It's been a long week," he sighed. "What did you want to talk about?"

"I'm pregnant," I blurted out.

"You'll have to get married," he said without cursing or raising his voice. I was stunned. *This was a lot easier than I thought it would be. Coming to the office was a good idea.*

"When do you think would be a good time to tell Mom?" I asked, feeling safe from his wrath and power.

"How can you tell your mother a thing like this when she is dying of cancer?" he said harshly. "This could kill her." His words pierced my heart and mind. He was more powerful than ever. No one had mentioned the possibility of Mom dying. I never realized I could make her die.

"Tell her later after you're married," he said, walking out of his office. As Jack drove us home I cried— for Mom. I was also upset at my father's insensitive remark, and the fact that none of the family had disclosed this with me. Jack's dad accompanied us to

Elkton, Maryland, to get the license. He drove us to a justice of the peace, and we were married July 23, 1966. When we returned to my house, Mom was in the kitchen preparing lunch.

"Mom, Jack and I have something to tell you," I said. "We were married this morning in Elkton, Maryland."

"Congratulations," she said. "I know you will make a good mother, Julia. Of all the kids, you were the easiest to raise; you took care of yourself and never needed anything." All my efforts to please Mom had been worth it. And without acknowledging, she had noticed them. I felt satisfied.

"It will be good for me to have you around," she added, "since you have chosen to be a mother instead of going to college." Wow, that stung. I was sure I could do both.

The family ate lunch with wedding cake for dessert—Mom had obviously been informed in advance. When I put the last of the plates in the dishwasher, the doorbell rang. Mom limped to the door and opened it.

"Please come in," she said to the woman standing there.

"Do you know this lady?" Mom asked, looking at me.

"No."

"I think she's our sister," Rosie said. She was right. My sister Connie, nine years older than me, stood in our front hall. It had been fourteen years since we were last together.

"I've anticipated this moment for years," Connie said as she looked at Jeannie, Rosie, and me. "When I became an adult, I returned to the orphanage several times, but Sister Spaciosa said she could tell me nothing of the whereabouts of my siblings.""However," Connie continued, "recently when I returned, Mother S. had been replaced by a new nun. She opened the filing cabinet and removed a manila folder, but she told me she couldn't give me the last name of your adoptive parents. As I was about to leave the office, however, she told me you were adopted by an Italian medical doctor in Chester, Pennsylvania. So I drove to Delaware County and looked in the phone book for names of Italian doctors in that area. On the third Italian name, I struck gold. I called your Mom, and asked if I could see you and your sisters. She agreed to my request."

She spent a half an hour with us. Before leaving she asked Dad if my brothers could come to see us as well. My parents agreed. It was a full day. I was trying to feel the wonder of marriage and Mom's approval; at the same time I resented my sister's timing because it distracted my attention from my marriage. I couldn't process and appreciate Connie's presence. I had put aside the notion of finding my siblings until after I became an adult and moved away from home. Then I would secretly locate them so Mom's feelings wouldn't be hurt. I downplayed my sister's visit so I could be loyal to Mom. I later learned this is called "divided loyalties," a dilemma common to many adopted children or children of divorce.

Two weeks later my brothers came to visit, I distanced them emotionally. *This is my family Mom had called white trash*. I glanced at Mom's face to check for hurt feelings, but she remained neutral and was cordial.

"Which one were you?" my brother, Allen asked. I felt insulted. *How could he not know me?* But truthfully I didn't remember any of them except for Ivan. When I left the orphanage, I completely forgot their physical appearances; I only knew they existed. Back then we were all children, but now my brothers were in their early-to-mid twenties.

Dad took them on a tour of the house and grounds. I guess he wanted to impress them with how well we had been cared for, but I felt guilty for what hadn't been in their lives. Connie and my brothers left for their home in Dalmatia, Pennsylvania, but not before Connie gave me her address and phone number on a slip of paper. When Mom glanced at me, I scrunched the paper and put it in the trash can.

CHAPTER 15: GOOD-BYES AND HELLOS

Throughout that year Alice's painful knees caused her difficulty with the steps. Leroy found a job as a truck driver, and they moved to Philadelphia. With their quarters now vacant,

Mom and Dad invited Jack and me to live in their place. Dad remodeled one of their bedrooms into a kitchen. Jack got a job at DuPont in Delaware, and I took care of my pregnancy. I never felt better physically.

Now that I was married, Mom treated me like an adult. She was in and out of the hospital more frequently. I sat with her many nights; while she was in physical pain, my heart broke with emotional pain. I maintained a "be brave, little soldier" demeanor, and I hardly left her side. My family taught me well how not to show feelings.

Dad was often unaccounted for, and Kathleen explained his absences by saying, "Dad was present when they operated on Mom. He saw that the cancer had metastasized. He knew she'd never be able to be his wife again." *Why wouldn't she be able to be his wife? She'll always be his wife.* I didn't understand what Kathleen meant at the time, but later it became clear that Dad said this to justify the two affairs carried on as Mom's cancer worsened. When Dad wasn't present, I stayed closer to Mom. While I held back the tears for Mom, I also held back my increasing anger toward Dad.

The baby was due on a Wednesday, but that day came and went. The next evening at 9:45, the contractions became closer together. My bag was packed, and Jack drove me to Sacred Heart Hospital. I was admitted and wheeled to a room with six other women in various stages of labor. During the night mothers-to-be were screaming; nurses scurried as they transferred women to gurneys and wheeled them to the delivery room. I watched and listened intently. Occasionally they measured me for increasing centimeters, then wheeled the gurney toward me. "I can help," I said. Raising my hips, I asked, "Should I lift myself over?"

After eight hours of labor, the baby was born at 6:45. Mary delivered the baby with no complications. She placed him on my left shoulder and said smiling, "Look at your new baby boy."

Since I was sedated, I didn't experience the screams I had heard from other women. "No, that's someone else's baby," I said groggily. "I didn't have mine yet." *It's just because Mary's my sister. She wants to give me someone's baby, and my turn hasn't come yet.*

"Yes, you did," Mary said. "Look at your stomach—you'll see." I looked at my stomach and noticed it wasn't as big. I looked to my left and saw a blue bundle. I gazed at his face and kissed him. I marveled at his tiny fingers and toes.

"What's his name?" asked a nurse.

"Andrew," I said. He was beautiful. I saw the creation and miracle of birth in his blue eyes. He weighed seven pounds, six ounces, and he was nineteen inches long. Mary had shown Andrew to Jack, but he never checked in with me. He went to work without saying anything.

Mom was admitted to the Oncology Hospital in Philadelphia two days before the birth, and I knew she couldn't be present. But Dad visited me and told me how pretty and healthy Andrew was. He asked if I needed anything, and I said, "Candy." He brought me three boxes of chocolates. That was the first time Dad personally bought me a gift.

Though fully awake and feeling good, I was disappointed no one had called about the baby. I called my mother-in-law. She asked how I was feeling but never mentioned the baby. Finally I said, "Well, how does it feel to be a grandma?" Only then did she realize I was calling from the hospital. Jack hadn't told his parents about Andrew, figuring he would just tell them after he returned from work. My in-laws came to the hospital that evening, and both looked adoringly at Andrew. Jack's mother gave me the book *The Prophet* by Kahlil Gibran. I thought his poem "On Children" was beautiful. It made a lasting impression on me.

> Your children are not your children.
> They are the sons and daughters of Life's longing for itself.
> They come through you but not from you.
> And though they are with you yet they belong not to you.
> You may give them your love but not your thoughts,
> For they have their own thoughts.
> You may house their bodies but not their souls,
> For their souls dwell in the house of tomorrow,

which you cannot visit, not even in your dreams.
You may strive to be like them
But life goes not backward nor tarries with yesterday.

You are the bows from which your children
as living arrows are sent forth.
The archer sees the mark upon the path of the infinite,
And He bends you with His might.
that His arrows may go swift and far.
Let our bending in the archer's hand be for gladness;
For even as He loves the arrow that flies,
So He loves also the bow that is stable.

The following day Mom surprised me. The Oncology Hospital allowed her to see her grandson and me with the promise that she return afterward. She entered the room wearing a mink coat and a woolen red scarf around her head. She had seen Andrew. "He's perfect. His complexion is rosy, and he makes a nice handful," she said with the biggest smile I had ever seen.

With Dad by her side, she presented me with a small box wrapped in silver paper. "This would be yours after I die, but I wanted you to have it while I'm alive and can give it to you."

I slowly unwrapped it, opened the lid, and saw a magnificent diamond ring. "The middle diamond is my engagement ring, and the diamonds on either side are earrings that have become too heavy for my ears. While you were taking care of me, I once told you that you earned another stone for your crown in heaven. But I wanted you to have these here on earth."

"They're so shiny," I said, holding the ring to the light. "I thought when you said stones you meant pebbles."

"Try it on," she urged. "How does it fit? I had the jeweler make it a size five." I slipped the ring on my finger.

"It's just my size." I gingerly removed it, placed it gently in the box, and told Dad to take it home for safekeeping.

"There may be times in your life when you need money, and you might think about selling this ring." dad said. "Before you sell it to anyone else, please come to me, and I will buy it back from you." They left my hospital room.

How could I ever sell this ring? It has been on Mom's finger for over twenty-five years.

The night before my release from the hospital, the nurse woke me to ask if I wanted a sleeping pill. "Why would I need a sleeping pill if I'm asleep?" I asked.

"Well, tomorrow will be a tiring day when you take the baby home, and don't count on sleep tomorrow night." She tried to explain that the pill would assure me that I would sleep soundly through the night. "Just take the pill," she said. "I have other patients to attend to."

The following morning I awoke with metal bars on the sides of my bed and my hands strapped down. I looked at my forearms and saw bruises. Mary was writing in my chart. "I can't move. Why am I fastened like this?" I asked.

"If you don't fight the bars, we can release the straps. But look at your arms."

"I didn't know I was fighting. Why are the bars up anyway?"

"In the middle of the night, you twice called the front desk. You told them you wanted Andrew dressed and ready to go home and to call you a cab. The front desk didn't know if you were someone wanting to kidnap Andrew, but they traced the call to your room.

"Last night a woman down the hall went crazy," Mary continued. "Because of your strange request, they thought you were hallucinating. As a precaution they put the side bars up, but you kept slamming your arms into the side bars trying to knock them down. So they strapped you in."

I recalled nothing. Mary ordered them to take the straps off, which they did.

A couple hours later, I had to pee. I rang for the nurse, but no one came to the room. *I really have to pee—to hell with this.* I climbed over the bars and went to the bathroom. I was climbing back to bed when the nurse entered. "What are you doing?" she asked.

"I had to pee, and that was the only way I could."

The nurse slid the bars down, and the hospital released me to go home that day.

I was a good mom, and Jack was a good dad. We lived in the house, but had our privacy. My parents did not interfere. I took two correspondence courses from Penn State to occupy my time. Mom worried I was spending too much time with her and not enough with Jack, But she needed me more, and Jack didn't complain. Andrew was a joy. Somebody said we didn't deserve Andrew, but I knew better. I truly thought his mild temperament was a characteristic of all infants.

Andrew seemed to boost Mom's spirit—from time to time I saw her smile. Kathleen had twins in June. She named one Karen and the other Kathleen, after Mom, which gave her more reason to smile. Mom saw another milestone when Rosie married in November.

In December Mom was admitted to the hospital for the last time. I visited her room and looked at her frail body. Cancer had robbed her of her looks as well as her spirit. She was in an oxygen tent with IVs in her arms.

As I sat with her, I thought of all the people who come to regret not telling their loved ones of their love. I unzipped the oxygen tent, not knowing if I was doing a bad thing. I stuck my head in and said, "Mommy, I love you."

"I love you, too," she said laboriously. "Why do you think we adopted you all those years ago if we didn't love you? Soon you'll be taking Andrew and going back to school. Then I'll have nothing to live for." I was nineteen, and we said "I love you" to each other for the first time. I didn't know until that moment that Mom had loved me all my life.

"Julia, call Joe," she requested. I phoned Dad and let him know that Mom wanted him to come to the hospital. When he entered the room, Mom spoke, but he couldn't hear her words, so I repeated them: "Joe, I've tried to be a good wife, and I never cheated on you. I've always loved you." Mom said no more. A single tear rolled down his cheek.

I comforted myself by thinking. *She's out of her pain, and this is what she wanted. She's in a better place.* Of all the people I've lost in my life, I miss her the most. Years later while enrolled in a course towards my Master's I wrote an assigned paper on "the person who influenced me most in my life," which follows.

Memories of Her

The thin, balding woman lay dying under the oxygen tent. Goddamn it! Why did it have to be her? She who was so good, so kind, and so young.

She had everything to live for. She had been closely involved in a very worthwhile project right up until this time—raising money for Crozier Hospital for the hospital to build and to expand—and there she was dying in the very building she was keeping alive. The hospital appreciated her. They unveiled a beautiful oil portrait of her a couple of weeks before and had it hanging in the lobby for all to see. She was someone to admire both inwardly and outwardly.

Before cancer had inhabited her body, she was a striking woman. At fifty years old, she could have easily passed for thirty-five. She had milky-white smooth skin, blond hair, and blue eyes, and she was nicely shaped. When she smiled, you smiled. She told me once—and I believed her because she only told me once—that she had a chance to marry Bill Haley (of Bill Haley and the Comets). She could have made it as a musician with her ability to sing, play the piano, and play the organ. She played both by sight and by ear. She used to play the organ on Sunday afternoon if nothing much was happening. I would sit next to her on the bench, never wishing to play but just content to listen When she played "Jingle Bells," I pressed the two bell producing buttons. Oh, I was great. She told me so. And when she played "Ave Maria," the entire house was silent and time stood still.

As she prepared dinner, she'd spend time playing cards with my sisters and me—war, poker, gin rummy, pinochle. She taught us how to cheat sometimes too. She'd play Scrabble with us, and we—especially she and I—would make up words and try to take the other's spot. "Did you know a-n-a-z-y-j is a weird kind of animal living only in the jungles of Brazil?" "Show it to me in the Scrabble dictionary," she'd say.

I would counter with, "It was in the edition before the one we have." Peals of laughter and a zero score for me and loss of a turn followed.

She helped us build a gigantic snowman one winter. We hid behind it, waited for my father to come home, and threw snowballs at him. She'd belly flop with us on our sleds down the windy, icy lane and pull us back up the "mountain" on our sleds. Although she taught us the game of hopscotch, she wasn't able to teach me coordination. She would draw the numbered blocks with white chalk while we found small stones. The one condition was that we would have to wash the chalk away before Dad saw it—that would make him mad because we marred the pristine landscape of the grounds.

She was the best Italian cook ever, even though she was Irish. She'd spend the entire weekend cooking for twenty or more people who would randomly appear any time on Sunday afternoon. She had exactly the right touch with seasonings and never measured them.

Mom was a cool hostess. She could welcome more than twelve hundred people who would come to a Republican rally on our grounds. She had done all of the cooking. We'd help roll the ham, cheese, and Lebanon bologna. She was gracious even to the slobs who thought nothing of flicking ashes on the carpets or looking through drawers. I was impressed when Governor Scranton presented her with a bouquet of roses—she deserved lots more of them.

Different projects or ideals she believed in excited her, and she never had anything nasty to say when someone did her wrong. She told me once, "At all costs be a lady." Bullshit. I have seen things blow up in many a lady's face. But she was a lady at all costs. Anyone who ever met her respected her. She was clearly devoted to my father. She was the main reason why we all saw him on a pedestal. She had placed him there from day one.

She could get angry at me though, and we did have tense times. When I was seven and preparing for my first holy communion, I was assigned to take a nap in the afternoon. I strenuously objected. While I was in the process of listing reasons why I didn't want to nap, Mom picked up a new doll I had received. While she was yelling at me to stay in bed, she broke the doll's head off and threw it across the room. I knew I had been bad. When I confessed my sins the night before, my soul had been cleansed of impurities, and I had just received the body of Christ that morning—now I already had a big black mark on my soul. I cried and apologized.

As I became the typically confused teenager, we had more verbal exchanges, mostly having to do with dating policies.

However, most of my memories center on her basic goodness. She wasn't a square—just plain, honest, and good. And she died in an ugly and painful way—something she did not deserve. And she who was such a beautiful person had been made to look wretched and haggard by the cancer that had invaded and spread through her body. It was unmercifully sucking all the good from her—her looks, personality, heart, body, mind, and soul. It won, and those of us left had lost.

She didn't give me birth, but she did give me life. She was my mother.

I received an A+ on the paper and a comment from the professor: "Why, why, why? Why this way? It had to happen, but why this way and why so soon?" Even today I ask myself those questions.

CHAPTER 16: A NEW BEGINNING

Mom died on December 19, 1967, which was the day that Jack and I closed on our used mobile home in State College. Jack's dad offered to go with him instead of me, but I rejected the offer. "There's nothing I can do here," I said. "The funeral won't be for a couple of days."

A month later Jack, Andrew, and I moved to State College. At that time, the presence of hundreds of thousands of American troops in Vietnam aroused protests around the country. I placed a flag sticker on the back window of our Ford Maverick that read "America, love it or leave it." There were peace marches and candle-light vigils on campus, but I had no interest or time to participate.

On several occasions the building that housed the chemistry department was locked due to protests against the Dow Chemical Company, the manufacturer of napalm, which recruited on campus. I viewed the protests optimistically. *Well the protests are a good thing since I don't have my assignment completed, and now I'll have another day to finish it.* Life was busy. Jack went to school full-time and had a part-time job at a gas station. Later he became a student assistant for a law professor who acted as Andrew's grandparent away from home. I started school part-time and worked at the Dairy Queen, which was across the street from the trailer park. We scheduled classes apart from each other so one of us could be with Andrew. Occasionally I'd tote him on my back to child development classes. He fit in well with the material.

We made friends with some of the neighbors who were also young students raising children. Occasionally one of us would have the other young couples over for food, music, and beer. The power trio of Jimi Hendrix was popular with a number of friends, but I preferred the lighter sound of Simon & Garfunkel.

I hadn't imbibed alcohol since before my pregnancy. since before I was pregnant with Andy. With our tight budget we didn't buy alcohol. So when I did have the opportunity to party, I would overdo it. Since Jack was not comfortable with socializing and small talk, he always went home early, but he urged me to stay if I wanted. Over time I developed physical relationships with two of the other students in the trailer park. I attached no importance to them since I didn't have feelings for either one. College seemed like the calmest time in my entire life.

Initially I had majored in journalism, but upon returning to school I changed to elementary education so I'd have the same schedule as Andrew when he started school. My grades were A's and B's. The only C I received was in Teaching Elementary Music where we had to play the autoharp and sing in front of the class. I had no difficulty learning the autoharp, but my vocal instrument had shut down years ago. While my sister Rosie received praise for her voice, mine was criticized, even by Mom. "Julia, you can't carry a tune in a bucket," she said. On another occasion I heard her tell company, "Julia's a monotone, and the only note she sings is flat."

When it was my turn to perform in class, I had trouble breathing. I froze, despite being told I would receive a zero for this part of the class. I thought that I would be laughed at, or worse yet criticized. This was my belief even though the professor was nice, and nobody laughed or made fun of anyone's performance.

In his freshman year, Jack majored in aerospace engineering because his high school guidance counselor had told him nothing else would be challenging. Jack never cared for engineering. During his first year, however, during his employment at DuPont, he discovered he liked business. Now back at Penn State, he changed his major to business and made the dean's list every semester.

Jack didn't know what he wanted to do after graduation, but he enjoyed being a student. When I was very young, I thought I would like to be an attorney. *Hmm,* I thought, *I don't want to be an attorney anymore, though Dad would have liked it. I know I've let Dad down, but he would be pleased if I was married to one. Maybe he'll make Jack district attorney.* I suggested law school to Jack.

He took the LSAT, scored well, and was accepted to Dickinson Law School in Carlisle, Pennsylvania. We moved to Carlisle, and I landed a job teaching third grade in New Bloomfield, twenty-three miles from home. Andrew went to preschool, and when he was old enough, he rode with me to attend first grade.

I took another job at the local Kmart three evenings a week in the grill to provide additional income. Fred, who also worked at

Kmart, visited me frequently on the job. He'd keep me company while I performed closing duties and scrubbed the grills.

I was flattered when he talked to me, especially when I found out he was the manager of the toy department. While other workers wore casual clothes, Fred wore a suit and tie. *A manager is an important person,* I thought. *He probably owns half the store, and here he is talking to me.* So when he asked me to meet him after work one night, I felt honored.

I followed his car to a side road, pulled over, and got in his car. He moved to my side of the seat and kissed me on the face and neck. He blew in my ear while he was groping me. He tugged at my panty hose, which I helped remove. I went into a trance and let it happen. When I was again fully clothed, he told me he was married but unhappy. I thought I could immediately make him happy. We continued to see each other for the better part of six months. One evening he told me his wife was getting suspicious, and then he broke off the relationship. I felt nothing.

I relished teaching the third grade, and the students enjoyed me. Even though I taught in a conservative school district, enough teachers in our building were in favor of an "open classroom" school. Now, instead of teaching only third graders, I would teach a mix of third- fourth- and - fifth graders based on ability grouping, which meant I had to step up my knowledge of mathematics.

I'd spend recess before math class with the principal and the head teacher on the day's lesson. " Help me," I'd implore. "This lesson has to do with moving decimals in long division." Or, "Mac, help me. This chapter is about converting fractions to percentages." We'd have a short lesson, and I was ready to teach for the day.

Mac was twenty-five years older than I was, and with his large build and bald head, he looked like Mr. Clean. He smiled, laughed, talked easily, and was optimistic. He was, however, unhappy in his marriage. He was fun. Sometimes we simply went out to eat without having sex. He sold *Encyclopedia Britannica* on the side, and I became a trainee. This gave us some time to be together while selling door-to-door throughout central Pennsylvania. I never made any sales. He was adventuresome and creative, always finding new places to meet. Once we met out in a snowy field. He had a blanket, wine, and cheese; we were at one with nature and our nakedness. We were compatible in our risk-taking.

These affairs made me question my relationship with Jack. *After all,* I thought, *Jack doesn't like to get physical, so these affairs are actually holding our marriage together.* When he wasn't studying, he was working. He never spent time with Andrew and me, and I didn't feel that we were a family. Andrew and I would go to the park, take car rides, or go to the lake. If the weather was bad, we'd play board games. When Jack didn't take classes in the summer, he still didn't involve himself with us, or anyone else for that matter. He seemed content to be alone. I took this as a sign of rejection, but also as a justification for finding affection elsewhere.

I began my master's degree at Shippensburg State Teacher's College—now a University—about fifty minutes from Carlisle. One course, The Well-Adjusted Self, was required for all students. We'd bring a blanket and pillow to class and learn about meditation and do trust exercises. I never volunteered to participate in the trust exercises (I was sure I wouldn't be caught in people's arms if I were to lean back). I was not able to stand with my back to anyone without having trouble catching my breath. In class we learned about self-hypnosis and out-of-body experiences. I tried this at home a few times, and I was sure I was on the roof of my trailer even though I was lying perfectly still on the couch. My mind was awakening.

I was often sad and became agitated easily. I wasn't getting anything out of my relationship with Jack. I began thinking: *There has to be more to life; there has to be more to marriage. It has to feel different to be a real family. This can't be all there is. I'm twenty-five years old and can't imagine another twenty-five years like this*. So I made up my mind that, when Jack graduated law school, in June I would leave with Andrew. Jack would do fine without us.

CHAPTER 17: LOOKING ELSEWHERE

Once a month another law student's wife and I went to the Walnut Bottom Tavern. We ordered a hamburger, French fries, and a pitcher of beer. We were about to order another pitcher when a man approached me. He looked intriguing with his wool herringbone suit, light-blue shirt, red necktie, and piercing blue eyes. I wore a Raggedy Anne smock top and blue jeans. I wished I had worn something different. He walked toward me and pointed at me.

"Do you want to play shuffleboard?" he asked. I hadn't played it before but hurriedly said, "Sure."

"I'm Elliot," he said.

"I'm Julie."

"Do you live around here?"

"Yes, my husband is in Dickinson Law School, and I'm a teacher. I have a six-year-old son. We live near here."

"My partner Ted and I are attorneys, and we're in Carlisle today campaigning for our senior partner who's running for Congress."He looked older, which gave me security. *Why is he talking to me?* I wondered. While I usually only drank beer, he ordered me a Galliano Stinger followed by a White Russian—then another and another. *Wow, I'm living it up, and these drinks all taste good*. After three hours Elliot took me to a friend's apartment. While Elliot may have had different things in mind, I was sick all night, much to the chagrin of the landlord. Elliot took care of me and cleaned me up. He drove me to my car around 7:00 a.m.. I returned to my trailer and stumbled into bed before the alarm was set to go off. When the alarm sounded, Jack turned it off and went about his regular routine. I got up and promptly called work telling them I was sick.

The following day Elliot called to see how I was doing. He asked about seeing me again; within a week, we met at a motel. He had brought wine and two fancy glasses. He told me that he was in the process of divorce, and I thought he meant he was already divorced. He had four children, who were living with his wife, and they visited with him every other weekend.

One weekend he took his children (seven to twelve years of age) to the Historical Museum in Harrisburg, Pennsylvania. We planned that I would travel separately with Andrew and we'd meet as if by chance. He introduced me to his children and told them that I was a client of his, making it look like a chance encounter. We marveled at how well our kids got along.

Another time he asked me to come to York and spend the night at his apartment. We ate at an upscale restaurant, and he ordered surf and turf for both of us. I hadn't been to a fine restaurant since senior prom, and I had never had lobster. Immediately it became my favorite food. We returned to his apartment, had drinks, listened to recordings of Roberta Flack and Carol King, and cuddled before going to bed.

What a romantic evening. So this is what I've been missing. We made love and fell asleep in each other's arms. This peaceful scene soon disintegrated when someone broke into the apartment through the bedroom balcony window. *Maybe his daughter needed to come over and didn't have a key,* I thought. At that moment a young woman hovered over the bed screaming at Elliot. He jumped up, and hurriedly ushered her downstairs, and addressing her as Hilda told her to leave.

I dressed quickly and fled downstairs. I saw she had knocked over much of the furniture and the Christmas tree. I grabbed my coat, but before I bolted out the back door, I heard her screaming, "How could you do this to me and in my very own apartment?" I dashed to my car and drove home. I was confused but was sure there was a reasonable explanation.

Elliot called the next day to apologize for the intrusion. He explained that Hilda was a friend and former client who couldn't pay her rent. So she had moved in with her mother, and Elliot had taken over the lease and moved into her apartment. Now I understood why she called it her apartment. *What a bitch,* I thought. *Here Elliot is helping her out, and she's causing trouble for him.* We continued to see each other, and she didn't bother him again. In January, Elliot asked me to move to York.

"I won't be able to afford it," I said, but thought about the offer more.

York seemed as nice a place to settle after Jack finished law school as any other. In addition, I already knew a person living in York.

"I'm not asking you to get your own place. I'm asking you and Andrew to move to an apartment with me, and I'll pay the bills," said Elliot, smiling at my naiveté.

"Give me time to think about this," I said. "I'll phone you in a couple of days."

This turn of events had me thinking seriously. *In June I'll be leaving Carlisle with Andrew, and I don't know where I'll go. But I'm certain I'll have a job to support us. Elliot's invitation makes a difference; maybe I can leave before June but continue to pay the monthly bills until Jack's graduation. I don't want to feel guilty about him not finishing due to finances.*

CHAPTER 18: THE GRASS MAY BE GREENER ON THE OTHER SIDE, BUT IT STILL HAS TO BE MOWED.

I left the marriage on a Saturday in February 1973. Although I had told Jack in advance, I believe he didn't think I was leaving. He didn't, however, ask me to stay either. We split the dishes, silverware, furniture, and pots and pans. The understood agreement was that Andrew would live with me and visit Jack every other weekend. I was glad the transition was smooth. I continued to teach in New Bloomfield, traveling a hundred and four miles daily until the end of the school year when I handed in my resignation.

One Sunday in June, I drove to pick Andrew up from a visitation weekend. No one answered the doorbell. I waited thirty minutes, and drove to a gas station, and phoned; no one answered. I returned to the trailer and waited. Finally I headed back to York where I phoned again. This time Jack answered.

"Where were you?" I asked. "I went to pick up Andrew and you weren't home. What time should I get him tomorrow?"

"I'm not returning him," he said calmly.

"NO!" I yelled, in the loudest voice I ever heard come out of me.

"Andrew's safe," he said reassuringly. Then he hung up.

I frantically redialed but got only busy signals. My world crashed. *Why would Jack want Andrew now when he didn't spend any time with him before?* It had never entered my mind that my child would be taken from me. In that moment I felt I was repeating what my mother had done.

Elliot was in California attending a conference. I spoke to him on the phone, and he told me not to worry. He would hire a detective, and we would get Andrew back. I felt assured. Two days later the detective gave Elliot the address where Andrew was cared for during the day while Jack worked at a law firm in Harrisburg.

Still in California, Elliot instructed me by phone to go to that address and ring the bell. When someone answered the door, I should swiftly go in, carry Andy to the car, lock the doors, and take off. While it was easy for Elliot to tell me of the plan from three thousand miles away, it was difficult for me to carry out. I practiced the plan in my head, arrived at the address, walked to the porch, and rang the bell. A woman at the screen door answered but did not open the door.

"I'm here to take Andrew home," I said.

"I'm sorry, she hesitated a moment, I was told not to give him to you."

"He's my son, and I have every right to him." Andrew heard me and ran out the door. I had him in my arms as planned and headed for the car. Just then Jack pulled up to the curb. The sitter had called him earlier because Andrew was running a fever. Jack grabbed Andy out of my arms and said, "I'm taking him to the doctor." I followed him in my car to the doctor's office. When I arrived at the office, I went into the waiting room where I confronted Jack.

"Why are you doing this when I have always taken care of Andrew?"

"Originally I hadn't considered taking Andrew from you, but a woman in York called to tell me you and Elliot went out for the evening and left Andrew home alone."

I was confused. "What woman? What are you talking about?" I was confused.

"She identified herself as Hilda and was telling me this for Andrew's safety. Then I phoned my mother who told me that I needed to protect Andrew." I remembered; Hilda was the woman who had crawled in the window the first night I was in York. In my haste to get away, I had left my purse behind. Elliot returned it, but apparently not before Hilda rummaged through it and noted my name and address. My son was her revenge.

"Andrew is *never* left alone. If we go out, he usually goes with us or stays with friends of Elliot."

"I've talked to him, and Andrew says he wants to live with me, so I have filed for custody. Jack explained that his mother thought it was in Andrew's best interests that Jack file for custody. Although Andrew was only six years old, he showed deep compassion for Jack. Later Andrew said, "Mom, you have Elliot. Dad doesn't have anybody." At twenty-five I didn't realize that a six-year-old should not be put in this position. I only saw Andy's caring nature.

Elliot was out of town for the custody hearing, and his partner could not represent me. Another attorney in York would not travel out of the county to appear in court, told me to represent myself. I went to court and argued before a judge for whom Jack had clerked previously. I lost and returned home devastated. I thought about leaving Elliot and returning to Jack, but I remembered my mother's words: you make your bed and lie in it. I was sure I could do nothing more about the situation. I picked Andrew up in Camp Hill every other weekend and the in-between Wednesdays. We'd go to dinner and then go bowling. In warm weather we'd go to a local park on Wednesdays where I introduced him to chess. I'd take him back to Jack's house, and I usually cried all the way home.

CHAPTER 19: THE BUMPS AND BRUISES OF OUTRAGEOUS FORTUNE

Soon after I moved to York, Elliot and I enjoyed a dinner at the home law partner and his wife. They had prepared a five-course meal complete with varying wines. On the way home, Elliot pulled into the city police station and remained in the car with the engine running. I thought perhaps he was dropping off legal papers, but he didn't get out of the car.

"What are you doing?" I asked. "The police could come out and notice that you've been drinking; then you'll be in trouble. Why are you doing this?"

"Shut up !" he yelled and backhanded me across my face, his blue sapphire ring hitting my eye. I opened the door, jumped out of the car, hurriedly walked to a pay phone, and called his partner. He came to the station within two minutes and talked Elliot into going home. The next morning I woke with a shiner. Elliot said he was sorry and explained it was an accident and only happened because he was drinking. I accepted his apology, and as we made love, I knew everything was OK.

If life had been boring with Jack, the excitement was just beginning with Elliot. His divorce was final. His ex-wife felt boxed in with the four kids and she wanted Elliot to take the children. We hadn't discussed this; the subject was never broached. We had Elliot's children every other weekend, coordinating their visits with Andrew's. I enjoyed the weekends but also the time between them.

Elliot talked about moving to a house in Dover, Pennsylvania, that his senior partner was offering for sale. *Why move? I'm happy where I am.* I liked our apartment complex with its clean, white design and new modern furniture. The complex included a swimming pool and social hall. A week later Elliot announced, without consulting me, that he had arranged for the movers to arrive that weekend because we were moving. Though I didn't care for this house, I had no other choice. The house in Dover was boxy, plain, on one level with a basement and out in the middle of nowhere. It had a kitchen, family room, living room, dining area, three bedrooms, and two baths. It was new, had no landscaping, and was close to the road.

Shortly afterward, his kids moved in too. They liked Hilda; and his oldest daughter, Bonnie, age thirteen, kept in touch with Hilda. They resented me and blamed me for things not working out between their father and her. Elliot's ex-wife was of no help; while she didn't want her kids full-time, she told them they didn't have to listen to me. They didn't. The honeymoon was over.

A month after we moved to Dover, Elliot wanted to have a housewarming party. He invited many people, including some police officers whom I had never met. On Wednesday before the party, a moving van pulled into our driveway and began unloading furniture. I opened the door and saw Elliot giving the driver directions to move the furniture to our basement.

"What's going on?" I asked.

"Nothing much," said Elliot. "The father of an ex-client kicked his son out of the house and since he could no longer live with him, he asked if he could store some things here."

"What was your ex-client charged with?"

"Federal bank robbery. But he was innocent. I got him off."

"He must have been framed," I said. "Aren't we remodeling the basement into a rec room for the kids? And aren't you having your party in the basement this weekend?"

"His stuff won't be here long. I'll have the movers place it in one area of the room." Then Elliot introduced me to his ex-client Arnold and his friend Reuben. *Another decision made without talking with me.*

I returned to the kitchen and washed the dishes. I looked out the kitchen window as the movers carried Arnold's beautiful furniture to the basement. *What beautiful furniture. Elliot's ex-client must be rich. Look at the quality and the amount and style. I would never figure this man to have a yellow crème Victorian couch. Price tags are still on the furniture. Poor guy—here he just purchased furniture, and his father kicks him out.*

Elliot passed me in the kitchen and said he was going in the bedroom to take a nap. Ten minutes later two men with drawn guns kicked in the front door. They barged in and pointed their guns at the "movers" coming in the back door.

One of the men yelled, "Put your hands against the wall." When they did, he handcuffed them. I knew Elliot had represented these individuals for federal bank robbery and they were acquitted. *Cops and robbers*, I thought. *You guys are playing this up a bit too much; they have to be joking with each other.* However, the man with the gun looked very serious and asked me, "Whose house is this?" When I told them it was Elliot's, the man said, "The attorney?" He looked at the other man in surprise. I led them to the bedroom.

"Elliot, wake up," I said. "These men want to talk to you." Elliot opened his eyes as both men showed their badges, and only then did I know the men were actual police officers. The one officer read him his Miranda rights and charged him with receiving stolen goods. Apparently all this furniture had been stolen from a local store a few weeks before. The police had kept surveillance on this moving van parked behind a barn in the neighboring town of Hellam and followed it to our house. Elliot knew nothing. At least that is what he told the district attorney.

The police drove him to the station where he was questioned and charged. The next day the charges were dropped, but the following day Elliot was arrested, taken to the police station, and fingerprinted. I was sure it was a setup. *After all the party was planned, and police were invited. Elliot would never have had police coming over if he knew there was stolen furniture in the house.*

"There's some mistake here," I told a detective who interviewed me. "Elliot didn't know what was in the van. We looked at some new furniture to buy. Maybe Elliot thought I had bought it and had it delivered as a surprise."

Although Elliot had not told me the true story, I tried covering up for him. He told me later that I shouldn't have talked to the police. His attorney said that my statement, since it wasn't true, probably went against Elliot. I was beginning to think that I was to blame for Elliot's troubles. That is exactly what he wanted me to think.

CHAPTER 20: THE OTHER WOMAN

While awaiting his hearing, Elliot worked less, drank more, and angered easily. I hid bottles of whisky or poured them out so he wouldn't drink so much. Midway through his legal proceedings, he'd left the house at eleven on a Saturday morning and did not return until Sunday evening. I was worried that something bad might have happened to him. I phoned many local bars. I phoned the hospital to check for accidents. When he came home, I was relieved. As he came in the door he said, "I just needed time to myself."

But the pattern repeated itself. So one Saturday morning I followed him and saw his car pull into a driveway. A woman came out of the house and greeted him with a kiss. I was furious. I pulled to the curb, dashed out of my car, ran up the drive, and confronted him on the spot. He told me to go home that this was his business and not mine. I was devastated. I drove around the block several times trying to comprehend and confirm what I saw. Each time his station wagon remained in the driveway. On my fourth trip around the block, the same woman who kissed him was in her driveway and shouted, "Come 'round the block again, bitch, and I'll call the police."

When he came home the next day, I confronted him again, "How could you do this to me?" I cried. "I have been here for you. I'm seeing you through this trouble, I'm taking care of your kids, and I'm looking after your needs." He punched me in the eye, and then he pushed me outside and locked the door. His oldest daughter was in the background asking, "Dad, why did you do that to her? Let her in."

"She stole money from me," he lied.

I went to some mutual friends of ours for help. They said they didn't know why I was ever with him in the first place and advised me to leave him. I slept there overnight. I called Elliot the next day, and he apologized. I returned home, and despite the bruises he welcomed me in his open arms. We made love, and all was OK.

Nevertheless, the weekends with the woman, whose name was Emma, didn't stop. *I still could have him if I just shared,* I rationalized.

I was numb and in extreme emotional pain at the same time. Closer to his trial, Elliot said I'd have to move out. It would not look good for him to be living with a woman, and the court would show leniency since he was raising four children alone. My heart broken, I obliged.

Since it was now summer, I didn't have a job. I applied for teaching positions in twenty-five school districts. At this time there was a glut of new teachers graduating, and with my master's degree and three years of teaching experience, no one could afford me. I looked in the want ads and found a job driving a truck for Skip's Foreign Auto, picking up car parts between Cumberland and York County. The owner put three-inch wooden blocks on the pedals to accommodate my height. My knowledge of operating a manual transmission paid off. Skip recommended me to an associate, and I kept the books for Gil's Garage. These jobs did not cover my expenses, so I applied for welfare and received food stamps.

As I worked these jobs, I kept checking the ads. I told myself, *you have a degree in teaching, but can't find a job, so you have to let yourself be open to other areas*. A vacancy opened up for a management trainee position at the Bon-Ton, a local department store. I was hired, no longer needed welfare, and gradually caught up on back rent.

One day I thought I'd surprise Elliot. I went to his Dover home to cook dinner before he arrived home. In the driveway there were two cars. The door was unlocked, so I entered. "Hi, Elliot," I called, "I wanted to surprise you, but you're already here."

The surprise was on me. I opened the bedroom door and found Elliot and Emma in my waterbed. Impulsively I took off my clothes and dove in bed with them figuring I was better than she in bed. I'd show her up. She was disgusted; she jumped out and went home. Elliot and I made love, and I knew that I meant more to him than she did.

Elliot and I attended the fiftieth birthday party of Mary, a friend and neighbor of mine. The doorbell rang, and Mary talked briefly with the person at the door. She called Elliot aside, whispered something to him, and he stepped outside. Curious, I opened the door behind him. Emma had crashed Mary's party. She was dressed in blue jeans and a fake ermine sweater, and her pink curlers were still in her hair. Elliot was trying to convince her to leave, but I intervened and got in her face. "How dare you," I yelled. "Who do you think you are? You're on my turf now. Get the hell out of here!"

Emma grabbed one of my hoop earrings and pulled it out, and I yanked two of her curlers from her head. Then she pushed me to the ground; on the way down, I pulled her legs out from under her. I got to my knees, hauled back, and punched her in her fat gut. With one single punch she doubled up. Mary appeared and ordered her off the property before she called the police. Emma left. Feeling pleased with myself, I went home, changed clothes, and returned to the party. I arrived in time for the champagne toast and secretly toasted myself. Only Mary, Elliot, and I knew what had happened, and none of us ever mentioned it again.

The next time I went to Elliot's house, I found that my clothes I had left behind had been torn up. The buttons were ripped off my shirts and the crotch cut out of my underwear. Elliot knew nothing about the destruction of my clothing and didn't believe that Emma might have had something to do with it. I no longer left any clothing at his house.

Two months later I discovered that I was pregnant, and I shared this information with Elliot. "What do you want to do?" he asked.

"I want to have the baby, of course." I said. "This child will be ours, and no one can take him away."

"That wouldn't be a good decision," he responded immediately. "I have my trial pending. It wouldn't look good if you were pregnant." Sitting next to me and taking my hand, he continued, "I'd like nothing more than to have a child with you. Our child would be beautiful and very intelligent. Not now—maybe sometime in the future."

I felt nothing. He was in the power position. I did not know I had a choice. When I had been pregnant at age eighteen, abortion was not an option. But within this circumstance I felt powerless. I gave paternalistic deference to Elliott. He gave me the phone number of an abortion clinic in Maryland, and I made the appointment. Ten days later he dropped me off at the clinic's door, went and had a beer and a sandwich, and later returned to pick me up. Other women were at the abortion clinic—some younger, some older. I was twenty-six at the time and felt dirty to be there. It seemed like an assembly line. The man in charge of positioning me on the table commented that even without seeing me standing, he would estimate from my leg length that I was just short of five feet tall. He was right. With what looked like a heavy-duty vacuum cleaner hose, he sucked the life out of me with a single loud swooshing sound. The abortion went fast, although not as fast as it takes to produce a life. I went in pregnant, and five seconds later I wasn't.

CHAPTER 21: A LOSS AND A GAIN

Elliot's trial was conducted during the Watergate era, when lawyers were very suspicious simply because they were lawyers. He opted to go for a nonjury trial; he was sure a judge would see the technicalities of unlawful arrest and the merits of his case. After two days of testimony, the courtroom was silent as the judge read his decision: "The court finds you guilty of receiving stolen goods. You are hereby ordered to pay the costs and fines of the trial. You are suspended from the Bar knowing in all probability your license will be taken away. You are sentenced to five years probation."

"May your soul rot in hell! I yelled at the district attorney You call yourself standing for justice. There was no justice in this courtroom today." Years later, however, after I heard the facts, I concluded otherwise.

Elliot made it seem as though nothing had happened to him. He still practiced law under the table; he just didn't present himself in court. This strategy worked until his ongoing cases were resolved.

He lived off uncollected fees, and over time he felt the financial drain. His children moved back with their mother because he could no longer support them. He put his house on the market.

During this period I worked at Bon-Ton in the manager trainee program. I began to enjoy living by myself without any drama. Three months into the job, I received a good review working in the women's department. After six months I did no better on my evaluation than I had at three months. My presence was requested in the personnel department. I felt certain there would be a raise, but was instead fired. "What!" I screamed. "I've never failed at any job. I've always put in my best effort. There has to be a mistake." I began sobbing hysterically. I was sure in the days ahead I'd receive a phone call and be offered my position again. No calls came; I collected unemployment and returned to transporting auto parts.

Elliot told me he would put in a good word for me with Jess, a friend of his who worked for the Lincoln Intermediate Unit, an educational agency that took care of children identified as having special needs. Jess was supervisor of the program for gifted students. Since I had my teaching certificate, he was willing to hire me in the event he needed another teacher. When fall came, however, an additional teaching position had not been approved. I applied as an aide in a classroom providing support for children with learning disabilities. I wanted to get my foot in the door. I had worked there two days, when the agency approved another teacher position for the gifted program. I was hired full-time with all the benefits.

Elliot renewed his interest in me. He phoned me frequently wanting to stop by in the evening. He liked the idea that I was a professional again. He completely surprised me when he began talking about marriage. I knew he maintained his relationship with the older woman, and another with the nineteen-year-old secretary of his former law partner.

One afternoon as I sat in my plush orange beanbag chair, Elliot knelt in front of me and asked me to marry him. "Julie," he said, "I want you to know that I've considered three women to marry, but I thought about intelligence as well, and so I chose you." *Wow! I won out over the competition, and all because of my brains.* I was on cloud nine.

CHAPTER 22: I DO

I delighted in picking out the pastel green paper for the wedding invitations. We were married in Maryland in late December 1977, to provide Elliot with a tax break. In January, we were remarried by a minister in front of people and had a small reception at the home of Elliot's former law partner. Life seemed stable. I was married, had a career, and was able to help Elliot feel better about his life. Elliot moved into my apartment. He didn't have a job, holding out to get one that was in keeping with his credentials and former earning power. He went to Washington, DC, where a friend of his who used to live in York was running for mayor in the DC primary. He commuted back and forth, but often stayed in DC for three or four days at a time.

Two weeks after our marriage, Elliot went to a workshop in Las Vegas for prospective political campaign managers. Two days into the conference, I received a phone call at 3:00 a.m. I recognized Barbara as the caller. She was the cousin of Elliot's friend running for office. "Oh, Julie," she slurred. "Thank you for being so understanding and allowing me to attend this workshop with Elliot. I'm in *our* room while he's in the casino, and I just wanted to call you. You must be a special woman to be so understanding."

I listened, not letting her words sting me. "No problem," I said. "I need to get back to sleep." Only when she hung up did I feel the full impact. *We've been married for only two weeks, and he's in Vegas with somebody else.* I shouted "No!" into the air and felt the echo vibrate to my core. This should have been a major clue that I had made a mistake. I cried and cried. I vowed not to talk to him when he returned. I'd show him through my silence that I was hurt.

He returned two nights later while I was asleep. He woke me with a gentle kiss. Once I was awake, he presented me with a beautiful card that was three feet tall. It had a love poem on it that began, "How do I love thee, let me count thy ways." All was forgiven. That was such a nice thing of him to do, I reasoned. *Well, she may have had him for a few days in Vegas, but I have him all the time.*

I knew he was depressed, I gave him the benefit of the doubt. I felt sorry for him. *Poor guy—his work identity was taken from him. He'll get over this stage.*

His candidate lost the election to Marion Barry, and Elliot was back in York full-time. Meanwhile his ex-wife sought support for their children and took Elliot to court. Elliot represented himself while his ex hired the attorney who had prosecuted Elliot. Judge Flannerly reminded him, "He who represents himself has a fool for an attorney. I order you to get a job, and I don't care what you do - wash dishes, sweep floors, whatever. I want you back in my courtroom, and if you don't have a job, you'll go to jail. Do I make myself clear?" he asked firmly.

Elliot found a job driving a truck and making deliveries for a local chemical company. He worked diligently and was a good employee. They realized he also had a brain, and soon he began working in the office. Now he had a sense of purpose.

CHAPTER 23: PROGRESS

Since teaching gifted students was subject to federal funding, I decided I needed more credentials to secure future employment. I chose to obtain my elementary school supervisor certificate at Millersville University. Although I taught during the day and attended classes at night, I applied for and was accepted into the school psychology certification program at Millersville.

As part of the psychology program, significant personal issues were identified—if we weren't willing to look at ourselves, we couldn't help others. To meet their requirements, I wrote an autobiography that offered a bonanza of issues for the professors to examine. The following week, Dr. Wilson, the professor, asked me to remain after class.

"How do you feel about what you've been through in your life?" he asked.

"My mother told me I'm an optimist," I replied.

"An optimist? Tell me more," he urged.

"I was thankful that I was adopted and didn't look back."

"But many negative events happened after your adoption," he noted.

"Yes, but I'd find positive lyrics or lines of poems, memorize them, and repeat them to myself when I felt down. Frank Sinatra sang a song with lyrics as follows:

"Do you remember the famous men who had to fall to rise again?

Just pick yourself, up, dust yourself off, and start all over again."

"And one day," I continued, "while exploring our attic, I found an old postcard in a trunk. And although I was only eight years old, it impressed me. So I memorized it and said it to myself when I needed a boost:

> It's easy enough to be pleasant,
>
> When everything goes like a song,
>
> But the one worthwhile,
>
> Is the one who can smile,
>
> When everything goes dead wrong.

"I'd recall those words whenever I felt like crying, and I practiced smiling no matter what happened."

"But how do you *feel* about your life?" he probed.

"I'm grateful I was adopted," I repeated. "My parents took me in when no one else wanted me, and I've had many opportunities: I earned my teaching degree, supervisory certificate, and am now working on my school psychology certification. My parents did a good thing. I'm the first adopted child in my family to complete college, and I'm proud of that."

While I was good at talking about my life, I presented no feelings. Staying numb and smiling always saw me through. The most difficult question I ever had to answer was often asked in my psychology classes: "And how do you feel about that?"

"But, how do you *feel* about your life?" Dr. Wilson asked again.

"How do I feel?" I repeated. "I feel with my hands. How do you feel?" He ignored my feeble attempt at humor.

"What do you *really* know about your family of origin?" he asked.

"According to my mom, they were "white trash."

"You wrote in your autobiography that your oldest sister searched for you, found you, but you and Jack were starting your life, and you didn't want to hurt your mother's feelings. Do you know where your sister lives now?" he asked. "She'd be a good source of information."

"I remember from her note that her last name is Long, I said with a smile, and her husband's name is Don, and they live in Dalmatia, Pennsylvania. I'll phone the long-distance operator. This is what I wanted to do since I was a kid. It's much easier to contact her now that Mom has passed. *I won't mention it to Dad or my sisters.* "I'll tell you next week what I found out," I said with a smile.

I drove home from class, put my books on the counter, and phoned long-distance. I was on a mission. Fortunately, Connie hadn't changed her residence. I wrote down the number and dialed immediately. My sister answered.

"Is Connie there?" I asked.

"This is Connie."

"Hi, Connie, I'm your sister Julie…er, Beverly. It's been a long time."

"Julie, it's so *good* to hear from you. It's been years. I'd given up hope that you'd contact me."

"Do you think we could get together?" I asked. "I'd like to know more about our family."

"Well, if you drive up you'll get to meet Mom, who lives with me now. I have six children, and I'd love to see you again," Connie said excitedly. "We'll have a reunion. Can you come three Sundays from now?"

"Sounds good to me."

Connie gave me directions to her home, and we said our goodbyes. I was surprised—for the last five years, we had lived only an hour and ten minutes from each other and never knew it.

At my next session with Dr. Wilson, he was pleased that I had followed through, and he was surprised at the ease of my contact with my biological family.

Another class that summer was called Encounter Weekend. It began on a Friday; but since no specific time was mentioned, my classmate Isabella and I kicked back, stopped at the outlets along the way, and had a leisurely dinner. When we arrived past nine, the rest of the class hurried toward us, and Dr. Howard was visibly shaken as he asked us where we had been. Isabella and I looked at each other.

"We've been to the outlets, I shrugged my shoulders and said, "the Robert Fulton Museum, and took the scenic route. We're here now—no big deal."

"The big deal is that the two of you have held up tonight's planned activities," he admonished. "We've waited on you to arrive to eat dinner."

"We already ate," I said. "But you all go ahead." Isabella and I sat at the far end of the table among glares. The dinner discussion centered on possible reasons why two students would delay arriving at an encounter weekend. We averted each other's eyes so we wouldn't laugh. For the rest of the weekend we played the role of errant children.

The weekend culminated on Sunday afternoon with Dr. Howard having an individual fifteen-minute session with each of us. He recommended that I enter therapy, and he gave me a business card with the name of his practice. He told me to make an appointment with "Tom."

I called on Monday and had my first appointment on the following Thursday. Tom asked me to tell him briefly about my childhood. I hesitated, wondering how to make my childhood brief. I told him of my upcoming reunion with my mother. He suggested that I meet with him weekly. When he rescheduled me, I said, "I did good, didn't I? I got through my first appointment and didn't even cry." In a later session, Tom told me I had a river to cry.

CHAPTER 24: AND THE TRUTH WILL SET YOU FREE

I told Elliot about the upcoming reunion, but he wasn't interested in attending. I was glad it was on a weekend when I had Andrew. The disloyalty to my adoptive mother entered my mind, and I couldn't give the title *Mom* to another person. Therefore I told Andrew we were going to meet his grandmother. Connie told me she'd have "Mom" waiting on the porch so we'd have some time together. "When you've had enough time," she said, "come to the back—we'll be barbecuing and playing yard games."

We rounded a curve in Connie's driveway and saw a wire-haired, overweight woman with flabby skin and thick glasses wobbling down the porch steps. I pulled the car to a stop, opened the doors, and prepared myself with a smile as we walked toward her.

"Hi," I said. "You must be Blanche."

"Beverly, you've grown since I've seen you!"

"Time has a way of doing that," I said sarcastically, keeping my distance. *What a dumb comment.*

"I wanted to keep you, I really did," she babbled. "I cried for three whole months."

I stopped her in mid-sentence, "It's OK. We're here now."

I introduced her to Andrew and asked Andrew to talk with her while I returned to my car to retrieve two pies. *Three months! Is that all I meant to you? How about the thirty years that I cried for you? I felt your absence every time someone asked about my "real" parents or whenever anyone uttered the word "adopted." And you cried for three whole months. What about the time I was ten and had angered my mother and she responded with "You can't make a silk purse out of a sow's ear. Your parents were white trash and you are too."*

"You're wrong," I insisted. "That's what you want to believe, and that makes you feel good."

"I'll tell you something else," she had yelled. "When you grow up, don't ever look for your parents because you won't like what you find."

My thoughts returned to the present. *And you cried "three whole months" for me. You can't be my mother, because if this is any indication of what else I'll be hearing, then my adoptive mother was right and I was wrong.*

I trudged to the porch steps carrying one pie. Blanche was talking to Andrew, and I focused my attention on him. "Isn't he good-looking?" I asked.

"I can hardly get over how good-looking *my* children are," she said. "Never mind the grandchildren."

"Andrew brought some pictures to show you," I said. I instructed him to show her the album while I got the other pie. *I guess you are surprised with our looks. What, did you expect us to look like you? God, I wanted you to be as pretty as Mom; I wanted you to be as smart as Mom. But you're neither, and what makes everything worse is I'm beginning to believe Mom was right. All those words and all those years I defended you amounted to zero or less. Time I could have spent making my relationship with her more meaningful I spent on you. I can't correct any of that. She's dead, and I can't give her the satisfaction of telling her she was right.*

I returned and placed the pie on the top step and sat between her and Andrew at a table on the porch. He was showing her a picture of my parents' house. "How's the weather in York?" she asked thoughtlessly.

"The weather in York," I said, "is the same as here—we're only an hour and ten minutes away."

"I wanted you to have a better life than what I could give you." she said, turning her head toward me. "The social worker told me that the person who adopted you was a doctor. Everyone told me that you, Georgina, and Nancy would have so much more there. Isn't that where you went?"

"Yeah, that's where we went. Everything was fine."

"They told me you'd have more clothes and nice toys—did you?"

"Yep, we had nice clothes and nice toys." *Marble statutes, marble floors, thick oriental carpets, a pipe organ, oil paintings, and a maid and a butler and a mommy and a daddy. But we didn't have you or dad, and therefore we weren't "real."*

Andrew was restless, and I took him to the backyard, met Connie's family, and returned to the porch where Blanche was smoking a cigarette. She smiled as she saw me return. I looked into her eyes, which were as blue as Mom's were but magnified by her lenses. "Tell me about Dad," I asked.

"He wasn't much taller than you. When I met him, he was a catcher for a softball team (*so was I ten years ago*) and he was ornery (*so that's where I get it from*). He was a great person when he wasn't drunk, but when he was, he was hard on you kids, especially the older ones."

"However," she continued, "you kids didn't have it near as bad as I did when I was growing up. I had rheumatic fever when I was seven and developed that nerve condition called St. Vitus's dance. I jerked all over, and the kids made fun of me, so I didn't go to school past third grade. I was close to my mother, and my sisters would tease me and call me Mum's pet. Mum died when I was sixteen, and that's when I met Alvin, your dad. He was ten years older than I, and the town drunk, but he talked to me and made me laugh. I didn't know I could laugh until I met him. He was the only person I felt close to other than Mum. My stepfather warned me to stay away from 'that little alcoholic,' and he told me that if he ever found out I was seen with him, I was not to darken his doors. I told Alvin what my stepfather had said, and your dad said it didn't matter; he'd take me home with him. He did, and he'd take care of me when he wasn't drinking. Those times were so nice—they made up for the other times."

"What happened to him when we went to the orphanage?" I asked.

"He left town," she said with a tear in her eye, "and I never saw him again. My world ended. I heard he died in 1963 of complications with influenza."

"If he were alive now, and you were sixteen, would you love him?" I asked.

"I don't need to be sixteen, and he doesn't need to be alive—I love him still, and I'd marry him all over again." *Maybe that's why so many people have said to me, "Don't you ever learn your lesson?"* Blanche snuffed her cigarette out and shuffled a deck of cards lying on the table.

"Wanna play cards?" she asked.

"Sure," I said. *That's why I searched for you—to talk about the weather and play cards.*

"Is war OK?" she asked.

"Sure, fine," I replied. *Is it ever going to be anything else?* "Wait," I said, "you just dealt that card from the bottom—that's cheating." *So that's where I got that from.*

"That's what your father showed me—he was fun," she laughed with twinkling eyes. For the first time in our lives, we laughed together. Somewhere in the laughter, her spirit emerged. War in cards is a mindless game, which gave me time to think. I realized that my adoptive mother had been wrong. My birth mother wasn't white trash—not now or ever. She was naïve and a victim of circumstance. She had replaced her "mum" with my father to have someone to be close to. She was just a very basic, under-educated, overly dependent person.

She had eleven children because that was what being close to her husband meant to her. When the authorities took us from our home and placed us in the orphanage due to child abuse and neglect, she probably did cry for "three whole months." She cried for my dad even on this day. She told me that, of her eleven children, my youngest brother Ivan and I were her favorites. When I asked her why, she said, "Because you both remind me of your dad—you make me laugh, and you make me think of him."

Blanche and I continued to play cards. I watched for cards dealt from the bottom of the deck, but was more aware of the cards that life had dealt my mother.

She was a confirmation of the capable, independent, caring, and giving person I am. Although I was born to her, I do not have to be her carbon copy. I realized my expectations of "Mum," as I now thought of her, were much more than she was able to give. I wanted much from her. I wished her to be a goddess, and she turned out to be just like me—a living, breathing human being, subject to all the frailties that go with the circumstances. My initial impressions of her were wrong. I had judged her harshly and prematurely.

Mum and I walked around the house to the backyard where Connie and her family applauded us. The barbecued chicken was great. I had an extra large helping of "humble pie." Before Andrew and I left, we arranged to return at another time when my brothers and their families would be there. She told me to invite Jeannie and Rosie.

Andrew fell asleep on the way home, which gave me time for reflection. *Mum's no more "white trash" than Mom was—different in many ways, to be sure. But each woman was merely a person giving and receiving from life what each one needed to survive.* I received what I needed on that day—the truth, not as told by Mom, or Mum, but the as felt by my heart and soul. That truth set me free.

CHAPTER 25: BACK TO THE BEGINNING

At my next session, Tom helped me process the day with my mother. He explained that as parents, we generally do the best job we can at the time given the circumstances. He felt that my mother was only being the mom that she knew how to be.

"Did you remember your siblings from the orphanage?" Tom asked.

"I remembered Jeannie and Rosie, who were adopted with me," I said. "I remember my brother Ivan when I saw him in the boy's line. However, I didn't visually remember the others—only their names. They came to the house where I lived when I was seventeen, and I met them all at that time, but didn't spend much time with them that day. I'll be anxious to meet them again."

"Do you have other memories of the orphanage?"

"I remember the rocking horse, red socks, the one nun only being nice some nights and other times being mean. I can still see other children playing together while I watched. There was a window ledge I liked to sit on and look out."

"Would you write your feelings about those times and bring it to the next session?"

"Sure, I can do that."

When I attended the next session, Tom noticed I wasn't freely offering the folded yellow lined papers I held in my hand. Finally he asked, "What do you have there?"

"I wrote some things about the orphanage," I said.

"Would you share them with me?"

"I don't know," I said, avoiding his eyes. "I feel funny sharing my writing. Maybe it's not what you wanted me to do. My handwriting isn't good, and it doesn't rhyme, and I probably could have done it better,"

"You're not getting a grade in therapy." Tom said, jokingly.

"OK," I said, "you can read this, but wait until I leave."

"You are the author, so only you know how to write it and how it should be read."

"I can't read aloud to someone, but I'll try," I stammered and read.

In the Beginning

A long time ago there was a place
Shrouded in gossamer veils
To hide the loneliness within.

The sheerness of the veil allowed
A faint ray to glimmer through
Focusing its light
On her.

Enough light to see out
To know that more light
Was available.

A little light was good,
What would more light bring?

More light is scary because

It is unknown.
The elusiveness of the veil
Taunted at her soul and at once
There was the longing
To throw off the veil
Yet cling to it—
It provided some cover.

Clothed her a little,
Kept her warm a little,
Could she dare expect more?
Who was she anyway and more,
What was she anyway, and more—
Isn't a little better than nothing?

She climbed into the deep seat of her well-worn red wooden rocking horse and sat. She rocked slowly at first, as if to assure herself she was still safe. The horse was her friend, and he'd carry her off to anywhere she wished. She rocked and rocked. She was the queen and those around her, her attendants. But she wasn't still and she wasn't playing—she was moving. Back and forth, back and forth. No, she wasn't hungry; no, she wasn't sleepy; no, she didn't have to go to the bathroom. This was her horse and no one else may have it.

The horse, the light
Both better than that within.
Light, motion, ever changing
Ever static.

The veil is not
so shrouded now.
The mist
Has lifted around it.
Still it is safe. Still

No one disturbs its silence

The source of the light was that broad window ledge—wide enough for one to sit on and wide enough to curl up and sleep on. Outside the window was more than inside. Look and look and look and then fall asleep happy. They came and lifted her off the window and she let them as if it was OK. But soon they'd leave, and then she'd climb up again to look out and finally fall asleep.

They wanted to take the light from her—
She wouldn't give it up.
They wanted to take her horse from her—
She wouldn't give it up.

Why were they taking these things from her? She knew the others didn't have these things, but they didn't want them anyhow. She wanted them, and no one was going to take them away.

She rocked and rocked and rocked,
And watched and watched and watched
And thought and thought and thought.
She felt good.

They lifted her from the horse even though she braced her feet firmly on each side of the insides of the horse. She screamed and they screamed, but they were bigger and carted her off attached to their side screaming and kicking. She wanted her horse. They wanted to clean her up.

She climbed to the source of the light.
The window ledge was high.
It didn't matter. She wanted it.
She looked out and there was more out there.
She wanted more.

Finally she was allowed back in the playroom. She went straight for her horse. But it wasn't there. They had taken it away, for she had made it dirty. She looked in closets. She found it—it had been removed to a room that had broken toys. A hand grabbed her arm and pulled her out; another hand slammed the door, and she could never get that door open again.

The mist is back
The veil has been draped back on.
She sits for longer times
At the window
And looks out.
She sits and rocks herself
And looks out.

No one lifts her gently off the ledge now. They are incensed that in spite of the barriers, she somehow still climbs up. They are at war with her, and they yank her down. She finds her way back to the ledge, but the ledge is no longer there. Bars are at the window, and not even a small girl can slip through. They think they won.

The thoughts spin crazily around.
Light and motion were the salvation,
Now they are gone.
She wanted motion,
They took it and made it motionless.
She wanted light,
They took it and replaced it with the gloom.

Was it too much to ask? To want?
Who was she anyway?
The veil was transformed into
A heavy black cloak and she was
Too small to take it off.

Tom encouraged me to keep writing.

CHAPTER 26: RE-REUNION

Connie and I planned a reunion for all of our siblings and their families. It was held at the home of Tom, my oldest brother. Tom and his wife, Sharon, lived half a mile away from Connie. Jeannie, Rosie, and her son Joey met Andrew and me at my home, and we traveled together. All of us—except for Alvin and his wife, Rose, who lived in Baltimore—had stayed in Pennsylvania.

At the reunion I had a surprise in the trunk of my car. I waited for the right moment when everyone was lounging and watching the kids play baseball in the field. Then I appeared behind my siblings and opened my super soaker. Water sprayed forth at whoever was in my ever-moving random aim. Screams and laughter followed. Then Tom rushed at me, wrestled the gun away from me, and soaked me good. More laughter. Good clean fun. *Had we ever had fun together?*

Andrew ran to me, "Mom, Mom, see those two kids," he said pointing to children appearing to be close to his age. "Their names are Tammy and Allen, and they go to my school. Now they're my cousins." My brother Allen, his wife Marti, and their children Tammy and Allen lived in Camp Hill, as did Andrew. As students, the cousins saw each other in the halls and at lunchtime but didn't know they were related.

Later that evening the older teenagers watched the younger kids while the adults walked down the road and into The Rendezvous, a local bar. One thing was for sure: we all liked our beer, and each was trying to keep up with the others. The jukebox played, and the rest of the family danced. Tom and I played pool. I had only played pool a couple times in my life, and it was sheer luck when I sank a ball.

"Tom," I said, "look at Rosie and Allen. They're dancing awfully close."

As Tom turned to watch them, I sank two balls with my hand. Tom didn't catch on at first, but when he did he laughed.

"I've got to keep my eye on you," he said, "or before I know it you'll win the game."

Then he called across the room to a friend, "This here's my little sister," and he proudly nodded his head toward me. I too felt proud that he was my brother.

Ivan and I played darts while others took over the pool table. Most of my darts sailed under, over, or to the side of the dartboard.

After it was last call and the music had ended, we paid our tab, left The Rendezvous, and zigzagged up the road. We retired to our sleeping bags.

There were a few headaches in the morning, and breakfast was more appetizing to some than to others. While my siblings and I sipped coffee on Tom's back porch, he and Connie shared information and experiences from our childhood before we were wards of the court. Tom's wife, Sharon, had photographs ready to share. Tom looked at Rosie, Jeannie, and me since the rest had heard these stories before.

"We all remained at the orphanage," Tom explained. "After Nancy (Rosie) was adopted,

the nuns were very strict with disciplining us with beatings and heavy chores. One day when I was fourteen years old, I retaliated by threatening one of the nuns with a kitchen knife. In 1953 all four of us boys were sent to a children's home run by the United Brethren Church in Quincy, Pennsylvania. When I was sixteen I was sent to a boy's reformatory in Pittsburgh , where I remained until graduation. and then joined the Navy. When Alvin graduated he moved to Maryland and married Rose, who he met at Quincy. Allen and Ivan later enlisted in the Navy and we all served on the same ship together."

"Since all the boys were leaving," Connie said, " Aunt Mary and Uncle Amos took me to live with them two days after you and Jeannie left, and I became their servant. When I was eighteen I met my husband, Don, and got married." *Finally, Rosie has proof that Aunt Mary and Uncle Amos truly existed.*

"What was our dad like?" I asked.

"Look over there at Ivan,"Tom said. "He's the image of Dad. And Julie, notice how much you and Ivan look alike? Dad was five three with dark-brown hair that curled in the center of his forehead. His gaze was piercing with cat-green eyes; playing the spoons and singing were interests of his. He worked in the coalmines of Schuylkill County. He liked to play softball and was a good catcher. His nickname was "Hap" because when he was drinking, others at the bar saw him get happy. Dad raised pigeons and did a better job of that than raising his children." It was true. Ivan, Dad, and I resembled each other. Sharon showed me Ivan's graduation picture. I had mine along to compare. We could have passed for twins.

"What caused the family disruption?" I asked.

"When Dad was drinking, which was every day," Connie said, "he became abusive. He had a gun and sometimes chased Mom around the house threatening her life. Tom and I took turns at the window trying to gauge what type of mood Dad was in when coming home from work. If he walked down the lane and had his gun pulled, the other of us would usher Mom out the back door and try to hide her in the woods. When Dad found out that Tom tried to protect Mom, Dad would beat him. The final blow, which led to a neighbor phoning the authorities, was when Dad broke a broomstick over Tom's back." Jeannie, Rosie, and I looked at each other, and I felt only sorrow and compassion at what my siblings had endured—*maybe viewing autopsies wasn't so bad after all.*

Connie looked me in the eye, "Julie," Connie looked me in the eye, and said, " I can't believe that you didn't remember my face when we were in the orphanage. I grew up feeling that when we reunited you would hate me for what I did to you."

"Hate you?" I asked in surprise. "Why would I hate you?"

"Whenever you messed yourself, I was in charge of cleaning you. One day Sister Spaciosa was so angry at you she told me to drown you while I had you in the bathtub. I didn't know what to do. I didn't want to drown you, but I knew I'd get a beating if I didn't follow her orders. So I wailed your backside, but you wouldn't cry and I had to hit harder until you cried out so Sister knew I was trying to follow her command. All my life I grew up feeling you'd have that particular memory of me."

"I'm sure I put up my invisible wall to survive," I said. "What an outrageously horrible thing to ask a child to do—kill their sibling! I feel nothing but compassion for you that you were put in such a position—you've had to carry Sister's burden for twenty-five years."

We hugged among a few tears. We took a break from the heavy conversation while getting refills on coffee and packing our cars. Then we settled on Tom's porch.

"I notice, except for Alvin," Connie said, "that we like our beer. While growing up there was often no milk in the refrigerator, but there was always beer. You three were weaned on beer," she said, looking at Jeannie, Rosie, and me. "We were poor and lived in run-down shacks. The floors in our house were indistinguishable from the yard—made of dirt and littered throughout with beer bottles and garbage. The difference between inside and outside was there was no dead grass or tall weeds inside. We didn't own a comb; our hair was often matted and crawling with lice. We were dressed shabbily in tattered clothes that were often too big for us. We were the kids other children taunted."

"Remember the night, Connie," Tom chimed in, "when you and I were trying to keep a fire going for heat? You, Alvin, and I stayed close to the flames, but Alvin's shoes were so ill-fitting that a live ember jumped into his shoe. Every step he took produced more pain. We looked for our parents from bar to bar, but couldn't find them. At the risk of exposing Mom and Dad's negligence, you told an adult at one of the bars the problem, and that person took Alvin to the hospital to get treatment."

"How could I forget it?" Connie questioned. "All ten of us had it rough."

"Ten of us?" I asked in surprise. "I thought there were just eight of us?"

"Two of our brothers, Terry and Lee, died as babies—Terry, I think, from a lung disease when he was four months old, and Lee died as a newborn when the cord wrapped round his neck and strangled him. Mom was home alone when she gave birth and couldn't help him. "Actually," Connie continued, "there were *eleven* of us. Mom was pregnant when we were placed in the orphanage. The baby—a girl named Jean-Marie—was taken from Mom at birth and placed with a couple in New York. When I inquired about you three, I also asked about her, but the nun gave me no more information."

Allen thought we'd spent enough time revisiting the past and suggested we go down the road to the American Legion and play pool and have a beer. Tom said he thought it was a good idea but not before he told one last story.

"I remember the time I looked for a sign of approval from Dad." Tom began. " One day I gathered scraps of wood, nailed them together, and made a doghouse. I was proud of my project. When Dad returned I was sure he'd be proud as well. Dad suggested that I be a dog and get inside. I crawled in and he told me to stay in the house a minute. He gathered a couple pieces of wood and nailed me in the doghouse. For several days he continued to nail me in the doghouse when he left for work and didn't let me out until he returned. Mom felt helpless to do anything and therefore did nothing."

"I don't remember anything bad about Dad," said Ivan, the youngest of my brothers. "He used to bounce me on his knee and sing 'Pony Boy." And after we were placed in the orphanage he'd visit.

As I sat in the aluminum webbed lawn chair, I felt blessed that I had been adopted, but I also felt terrible guilt that I hadn't spoken up for my siblings. *What pain and humiliation I might have saved them.* In true Stauffer fashion, we made our way to the American Legion and raised our beers. I proposed a toast: "Hear, hear, we raise our beer to Mom and Dad and all their cheer." Before we loaded the car to go home, we posed for photos positioning ourselves as if we had been on the steps of the orphanage twenty-five years ago.

CHAPTER 27: EMERGENCE

My life was stable, and I had urges to be a mommy again. I wanted a child who would never have to go between houses, who would be all my own, and who no one could ever take away. I had my tubes tied shortly after the abortion when all of Elliot's children were living with us. I felt I did my duty to motherhood and was sure I would never want to have children again.

In February 1979 Elliot and I went to Hotel Hershey for a sweetheart weekend. I saw a family at the pool who had two adopted Korean children. They looked like a happy family where nothing ever went wrong and everything was good. I wanted that type of family.

On the drive home from Hershey, I proposed my idea of adoption to Elliot. He was tentative but saw nothing wrong with me researching local adoption agencies. I discovered there was a two-year waiting period to adopt a baby. In my search I came across the Gibbons Agency, which placed hard-to-adopt children such as a minorities, multiple family members, physically or mentally handicapped children, and older children. We applied to adopt, attended classes, and had a home visit performed. The last assignment was to write an autobiography. We completed everything but the waiting.

We moved from my apartment into a fixer-upper house in York City. It was a three-story brick row house, which we planned to remodel. With its three bedrooms, there would be space for visiting children as well as a permanent child. The house required a new kitchen and bathroom, and it needed to be repainted and wallpapered throughout. It had an old coal furnace, and coal was delivered from a truck that positioned its chute into the front cellar window. We were optimistic. We'd make this house into a home for our family. So we spent evenings and weekends rehabilitating the house while living there.

Before the house was finished, we received word from Gibbons that a seven-year-old boy from Korea was available. Initially I had thought about a baby. But a little boy made sense; he would be school age, and we could still work and meet his needs. Our son Benjamin arrived in Philadelphia in July 1980. We met him at the airport, watching anxiously as the passengers departed. No little boy came out with the other passengers and I was getting nervous. Other children departed the plane but they were all girls. Then I saw him. He was playing with a tiny plastic airplane pretending to be flying it around the airport, but because his hair was shoulder length, I mistook him for a girl.

I went to him and said, "Benjamin?"

"Ooma? Appa?" he asked, meaning *mother* and *father* in Korean. We had sent him a scrapbook of ourselves, and he recognized us. We sat down to have a soda and looked through the book together, thinking and speaking in two different languages and many smiles.

His chaperone had been busy inquiring at the information counter about our whereabouts. When he spotted us at the airport restaurant, he greeted us and had us sign the papers signifying he had turned Benjamin over to us. He left hastily.

On the ride home, Benjamin said, "Ojoom." I smiled and said "ojoom" back to him, and he nodded his head. This exchange continued until he said "ojoom" with an unmistakable urgency in his voice. We stopped at the closest bar, and Elliot took him to the bathroom.

Ben was an absolute delight. He acquired English quickly and adapted to a routine. Since it was summer, I didn't work and only had my psychology courses, so Ben and I hung out. I took Ben to one of my therapy sessions since I wanted reassurance from Tom that I was parenting correctly. During the session Benjamin jumped from place to place. I stooped to his level, made eye contact, and firmly said, "No!" Tom told me I was doing a good job setting limits. Benjamin listened and busied himself playing with toys on the floor. There was little need for discipline, and he responded well to verbal correction. His temperament charmed us.

I began thinking *he'll be spoiled if we bring him up as an only child.* Andrew could visit only every other weekend. Elliot's kids were older and didn't visit anymore. Therefore I talked again about adopting a sister or brother for Ben. We asked the agency about another child. This time they showed us a picture of a nine-year-old girl. She looked alone, although there were other children in the background. I felt lukewarm toward her, but we went ahead since she was close to Benjamin's age.

Ais Hi arrived the following January. We drove to Kennedy airport in a snowstorm but met her plane on schedule. She came off the plane carrying two brown paper bags with handles. Her whole life was contained in those bags. She had a beautiful silk ceremonial Korean dress with her, ten little books of children's classics written in Korean, a doll baby, and a Korean bible. She gave us a big smile, but other than that was reserved. We thought that Benjamin could help with the language:

"Ask Ais Hi if she has to go to the bathroom," I requested.

"You, bathroom?" he asked. He had forgotten his Korean language. Ais Hi ignored him, but more alarming she seemed disinterested in him. Benjamin looked hurt. I chalked it up to a twenty-three-hour flight. We stopped briefly at an airport restaurant, but Ais Hi ate nothing. Benjamin had no difficulty eating her hamburger and French fries.

We walked to the car preparing for the long ride home. The car wouldn't start because the battery was dead. I took Benjamin and

Ais Hi inside the airport while Elliot went to get help. Once inside, Ais Hi was active. She raced into a store and pointed from shelf to shelf, object to object. She wanted it all. I took her by the hand, led her out of the store, and found a quiet space on the floor where she, Benjamin, and I sat.

I had brought some books, drawing paper, and crayons along to occupy Benjamin in case we had to wait for the plane to arrive. I removed the drawing paper and crayons from the canvas sack and handed them to Ais Hi. Ais Hi immediately began drawing. Her work was incredibly detailed. She drew a woman in a beautiful formal gown with hair piled on her head. She wore diamonds and pearls around her neck and rings on her fingers. She had lace around the edges of the hem of her dress and lace at the end of her sleeves. Ais Hi handed the drawing to me. For all the details she had drawn, oddly there were no facial features. *Maybe she just hasn't finished*, I thought. However, she continued producing drawings that all lacked facial features. I knew from my psychology class on projective drawing techniques with children that the absence of facial features signified an inability to relate and interact with others, and the abundance of material goods represented superficiality. I was concerned.

Elliot returned to the airport. The car battery was charged; we packed the supplies and headed to the car. It had been a long day, and at least three of us were weary. Benjamin slept. Ais Hi began to sing. Her voice was beautiful. She could reach high notes with ease. She sensed we liked this from our smiles and continued from one song to the next. I was truly in awe of her talents.

We had left the Christmas tree up originally thinking Ais Hi would be with us for Christmas. There were packages under the tree with her name, and I pointed them out to her. She immediately went for them, unwrapping furiously. Benjamin moved in closer to see her things, and she got up and pushed him out of the way. I corrected her in a stern voice, "No!" But she totally ignored me. When we finally went to bed, I had mixed feelings about Ais Hi. She was obviously a very intelligent, artistically gifted child, but I couldn't get her pictures without any facial features out of my head.

The next day I registered Ais Hi at our neighborhood public school. Ferguson was one of the York City Schools where I was the school psychologist.

From the outset I heard how bright Ais Hi was from her teachers, but they too had concerns about her personality. If someone brushed up against her, she interpreted it as an attack and became dramatic, yelling and crying about how the other student had hurt her.

Ais Hi tended to think she was better than others, and she did not relate to her peers.

Power struggles abounded at home. I was determined that Ais Hi was going to be "one of the kids." She insisted on getting dressed up for school. Day after day I'd send her back upstairs to change into jeans or a casual skirt. She put her patent leather shoes in her book bag only to change at school. She set herself up to be teased by her classmates and continued being arrogant toward Benjamin; he began to stand his ground.

I saw through her manipulation and brought it to her attention. Elliot began to side against me in her presence, which she used to her advantage. Whenever I corrected her, she'd go to Elliot for sympathy. The arguing with Ais Hi and Elliot over this issue increased. Ais Hi isolated herself, spending increasing amounts of time in her room. It got to the point where I'd discipline her by having her spend time out of her room. She learned that by putting on a long face, Elliot would allow her to retreat to her room.

Sometimes when I'd put her in time-out, Elliot would come home and, not knowing the circumstances of her time-out, tell her she could get off the chair. I felt hurt and had resentment toward him and Ais Hi. I knew these techniques were sound, but he wasn't giving them a chance to work, and he was not allowing me to have credibility as her mother. Elliot was questioning and sabotaging my authority. I felt a double rejection. He was choosing her over me, and she was choosing him over me. And what's more they were doing this together. I felt helpless. To avoid the feelings of rejection, I became more involved outside our home. With two children at Ferguson, I joined the PTA and eventually became the president. The positive activities with other parents, teachers, and children reinforced my abilities.

Sometimes to lessen the tension on a weekend, we'd drive to Lake Meade to enjoy boating, swimming, or fishing. I'd pack the picnic and add a six-pack of beer. Elliot would fasten our small sailboat to the boat trailer. Benjamin and Ais Hi had rolled their swimsuits into their beach towels, and off we'd go to enjoy some leisure time at the lake. Since we all enjoyed the water, the trips were usually carefree. However, one hot Sunday afternoon when Elliot, Ais Hi, Ben, and I were at the lake, the kids had eaten and were reading in the shade. Elliot and I launched the boat onto the lake. However, a tricky wind arose due to our inexperience, making it hard to work together. After fifteen minutes of arguing, I became frustrated, jumped off the boat, and swam to shore. Elliot sailed to shore, returned the boat to its trailer, and drove away with the boat, our clothing, and the food. *He's going to get more beer, I thought.* and I reassured the kids that he'd be back shortly.

After an hour it became clear that he wasn't coming back for us. I told Ben and Ais Hi that, if we started walking, we would probably see him returning for us. We walked barefoot and in our swimsuits. A couple of cars passed us; embarrassed by the situation,

I didn't ask for help. About six miles into our walk, it was getting dark and not safe to continue walking. I stopped at a house with lights on. I told the couple that my husband had been called away on an emergency and hadn't returned for us. They let me use their phone to call Elliot, but there was no answer. The owners of the house were compassionate and drove us home.

When we arrived home, our car was in its usual parking space. I called out for Elliot, but received no answer. He was sound asleep in bed. Although I was furious with him, I also knew not to awaken him since he handled confrontation when he was inebriated by being physically abusive. I bathed the children and put them to bed. I bunked on the couch for the night. The next morning at breakfast, I asked Elliot why he left us. He said he didn't remember doing that but he was sorry if he did. No one mentioned the incident again.

CHAPTER 28: SETTING BY EXAMPLE

I kept in touch with my siblings, and we'd get together at least once a year, or more, for a special event. With all of Connie's kids, there was usually a wedding. The summer after Ais Hi arrived, Connie's son Russ married. Elliot, the kids, my brother Ivan, and I traveled to Millersburg, Pennsylvania, to attend Russ's wedding. The adults drank beer along the way. We stopped at Connie's house, which was a mile away from the church, but she wasn't home. Her door was unlocked; so we all entered and used her bathroom. Ivan and Elliot turned on the TV to watch a baseball game. The wedding was due to start in thirty minutes.

"It's time to go to the church," I said. Elliot and Ivan remained in their chairs.

"Get in the car," I said, looking at the kids. Benjamin started for the door, but Ais Hi didn't move. I was annoyed at Elliot and Ivan.

"When I tell you to get going, I mean it. Get going!" I said, looking at Ais Hi.

"Don't talk to her like that!" Elliott yelled as he charged at me.

My lip was bleeding and my pant knee was torn and blood-stained. I hurried out the back door of Connie's house and took the kids to the wedding. At the reception I explained my appearance with the lie that I had slipped on the gravel in the driveway. I was embarrassed to tell the truth.

After the reception, I drove back to Connie's and sent Benjamin into the house to tell Elliot and Ivan it was time to go home. Neither acted as if anything had happened, and they didn't ask about the wedding. On the way home Elliot slept in the back seat.

I said to Ais Hi, "Never let a man treat you like the way I was treated today."

CHAPTER 29: JOY

One day in January 1982, I volunteered at the adoption agency, I saw a picture of a sad-looking, two-year-old girl in Korea named Astral who was available for adoption. I looked at her birth date and noticed it was the same as mine—obviously a true sign that she was meant to be with us. Elliot was not happy with the prospect of adopting a two-year-old, but I was excited, and so was Benjamin. Ais Hi couldn't have cared less.

Benjamin and Ais Hi's naturalization ceremony occurred before the baby arrived in April. We gave them the opportunity to choose a different first name. Benjamin thought about Christopher but decided to remain Benjamin. Ais Hi chose Jan Lee.

Astral, whom we later called Lilly, was petite with jet-black hair and almond eyes. She weighed only twenty-three pounds although she was over two years old. She was still in diapers, and was my first baby since Andrew. She was a wonder with a good disposition. She and Benjamin bonded immediately because she reminded him of the young kids he had helped care for in Korea. He knew how to change a baby quickly. Lilly bonded with both Elliot and me. She went to the YMCA day care program until the summer when she could be home with her siblings and me. On any given summer afternoon, Ben would pack a lunch, put Lilly in his red wagon, and wheel her to the park.

The centennial of Korean-American diplomacy occurred in 1982. Elliot and I received an invitation to attend a party on May 15 hosted by the Korean Association of Central Pennsylvania. We were the only Americans there. The emcee asked Elliot to draw the ticket for the grand prize, a two-week trip to Korea. He read the number: "Nine, zero, zero, two, three." I checked my ticket as Elliot read the number again. I raised my ticket in the air—I was the winner! The emcee was gracious and told the disappointed crowd that this outcome was appropriate since we had adopted three children from Korea and we were American. The other attendees glared at me as Elliot and I led the final dance of the evening. But there was a Korean woman named Yung who told me she was going to Korea in July to visit her sister. She said that if I wanted to go with her, she'd help me navigate the airport and safely get to where I needed to be. She would talk to her sister and see, if maybe, I could stay with her for a week. She gave me her number so we could make plans.

The prize only covered airfare, and the trip had to be taken by the end of the summer. Although I didn't want to leave the kids for two weeks, I'd have the opportunity to see Seoul, where Jan Lee was from, and Pusan, where Ben and Lilly were born. I'd also get a chance to visit the Eastern Welfare Agency and perhaps find out more about the children's background. *Maybe they won't have to wait until they're adults to find more information,* I thought.

I decided it was a good idea to live with a Korean family because I wanted to get a feel for what the kids went through when they arrived in America and didn't speak the language. I flew to South Korea in July. The flight lasted twenty-three hours, and we arrived late in the evening. With Yung to interpret, I had no difficulty getting through customs. Friends of Yung met us and asked us to join them at a nightclub. I just wanted to rest, so I checked into a local hotel' where Yung agreed to meet me the following morning.

I took a hot shower and promptly fell asleep. I awoke feeling very thirsty. I went to the hotel lounge, which was located on the top floor and provided a breathtaking view of Seoul. I sat at a table by the window with my journal and travel brochures, and I ordered a beer. Two men approached my table, one of whom spoke English.

"Are you alone?" he asked.

"Yes, I'm visiting your country," I said. They looked around the room to make sure I was alone and then sat down at my table.

"What is your business here?" he asked.

"I have adopted children who are from Seoul and Pusan," I said, taking pictures from my wallet. "I want to get to know their country."

The one man smiled at the other and said something in Korean. They both looked at me as the one interpreted.

"He wants to know if you press for money?" *They must think I do laundry.*

"Press for money? I don't even iron at home, let alone on vacation."

"Let me say it in another way," he said smiling. "Do you couple for commission?" *It's sinking in; they think I'm a prostitute.*

"No, no," I said pointing to the pictures of my children. "I'm from America—these are my children—and I'm going to Pusan from here."

"My friend wants to know if you'll go as his traveling companion to Pusan for two days. He will pay all expenses, and he will give you one hundred dollars a day."

"No, I don't do *that*." I shook my head for emphasis. But the one man looked angry.

"OK, now he says one fifty," the other said.

'No, it isn't about money; I'm not a prostitute."

"Why are you here alone? Women don't go to bars alone unless they couple for commission." Ordinarily, I'd be amused by this conversation; however as I read their expressions and heard their raised voices, I knew they were serious. I didn't feel safe, but I was in their country.

"OK," I said "tell your friend I will meet him tomorrow morning at ten." He relayed the message to his friend who smiled at me. Then they both left my table and the lounge. I knew I'd be checking out at 8:00 a.m.

Yung met me on time, and I was glad to be leaving. Her brother drove us to her sister's house, where I unpacked and gave her family gifts. The house was spotlessly clean, and soothing cooking aromas filled the air. The family welcomed me. They were "middle class" but slept on grass mats on the floor. I walked around the neighborhood and found my way to a corner store where I spotted Coca-Cola—a taste of home.

Kim chi, a staple of the Korean diet, overpowered my senses of smell and taste. It is made from cabbages that are layered with hot peppers, garlic, scallions, and onions and then cured in five-gallon crocks that are buried in the ground for months. Kim chi accompanied *every* meal, even if the meal began at 5:00 a.m. Once dished from the crock, it was stored in Tupperware containers for easy access for the rest of the day.

Yung arranged for sightseeing the first week I was in Seoul. We went to the Seoul Tower, which at 479.7 meters above sea level was the highest tower in the East. We rode the suspended cable car to the top and walked down. Seoul is a city of nine million people with one-fourth the area of New York City. Its contrasts are stunning. Amid the skyscrapers are humble Buddhist temples where many people visit throughout the day to meditate.

From Seoul I traveled by bus to Pusan, and spent the next two days there. Seoul. Pusan is a seaport city, much less dense and more laid back than Seoul. I viewed the local markets that Benjamin had talked about. There were many alleys with little shops. I saw a little girl about Lilly's size toddling around her mother's fruit stand and drinking coffee. Lilly would say "kopi" and point to Elliot's coffee. I thought she had her *p*'s and *f*'s mixed up, but *kopi* is the Korean word for coffee. Since Pusan is a seaport city, Yung and I had talked about relaxing on a beach, but the rain was torrential from the time we arrived. An umbrella she purchased on arrival lasted two blocks before turning inside out.

By the second week, I was homesick. I missed my family, the English language, and American food. *This must have been how my children felt upon coming to America.* I made the decision to leave the Korean family, and I checked into the Westin Chosun Hotel in downtown Seoul. On my first day at the Chosun, I signed up for a tour of Kyongbok Palace, which once housed royalty. In the hotel lobby, I met other international tourists, and I introduced myself to a couple from Sweden who were picking up their six-month-old daughter to be adopted. We compared pictures of our children, and I asked,

"By any chance is your baby from Eastern Child Welfare?" I asked.

"Yes, that's where our baby is," the Swedish woman said. "We are going tomorrow morning to receive her."

"Could I possibly ride along?" I asked.

"Sure. Meet us in the hotel lobby at nine thirty."

The next morning, we met and took a taxi to the hospital. The adoption department was on the seventh floor. The couple went on their way, and I asked for Mr. Kim, who was head of the agency. The receptionist told me I had the wrong agency. I was at the Social Welfare Society, not Eastern Child Welfare. The receptionist phoned Mr. Kim, who said I'd have to know my children's case number to arrange an appointment with him.

I returned to my hotel disappointed, but I knew the case numbers were just a phone call away. I called Elliot, who seemed pleased to hear my voice. He told me that Benjamin and Lilly were both up and dressed for swimming and that Lilly was standing on a stool beside him singing a song. My guilt of leaving her so soon after her arrival eased; if she was singing, she must be happy.

I called Eastern Child Welfare and gave them the case numbers. Mr. Kim informed me that only Benjamin and Lilly came from his agency. He arranged an appointment with me later in the week.

On Friday morning I hailed a cab. I gave the driver the address written on a piece of paper. Although he shrugged his shoulders, he consulted with two other cab drivers, an affirmative nodding of heads. He drove for fifteen minutes, and the traffic thinned. Then he pulled over to the side of the road, talked with a local person, and made a U-turn. We had reached our destination since the sign on the building was marked in both Korean and English.

I went to Mr. Kim's office on the third floor and introduced myself to the receptionist, Maria Cho, who was the woman I had spoken with on the phone. She informed me that Mr. Kim was not in. She apologized that the agency hadn't sent a car to the hotel for me. Maria introduced me to a woman who turned out to be

Lilly's caseworker. Her file contained no more information other than what we had received. I brought her up to date on Lilly's personality and development. Another woman entered the room who had been Benjamin's caseworker. She remembered him and talked about him. I gave her the plant holder that Benjamin had asked me to give to a boy in Korea. The caseworker showed it to the office staff, who I thought smiled in appreciation. *Benjamin can make people smile over any distance.* I left updated pictures of them for the staff to enjoy.

A couple children in the office were waiting for a flight to America, but their flight was delayed because of a typhoon. "Each child comes here only for processing," Miss Cho said. "Then they are sent to a foster home. It is only the older ones who go to the orphanage."

As I was leaving the agency, Mr. Kim returned and escorted me to his office. We sat and talked of the kids, of adoption in general, and of the assimilation of Korean children in America. He was pleased to hear of the high adjustment rate and acceptance into American society. Then Mr. Kim surprised me by asking me to join him and his staff for lunch.

"My only concern," he said, "is that you may not like Korean food."

"No problem," I said. "I am honored to have lunch with caretakers of my children."

He drove me to a restaurant where his staff had arrived before us. As we entered the lobby, the staff applauded us. Among his staff was Dr. Kim (not related to Mr. Kim), a pediatrician who remembered Ben and Lilly. I felt an immediate connection with her.

"We are honored to have you as our guest," Mr. Kim said turning to me. "This is not our usual fare—this is a meal reserved for royalty." He escorted me into the dining room arm-in-arm, and everyone else lined up behind us.

This was my best meal ever (besides Mom's spaghetti). As I sampled each dish, I had only one disappointment. The crabs looked enticing smothered in a hot red sauce, and by now I had learned to eat rice to balance the spices. One bite into the crab and I discovered that it was raw. I gave mine to the woman to my right who readily ate it, much to Mr. Kim's disapproving looks.

Dr. Kim differentiated between the two types of noodles. "These are plain noodles," she said in perfect English. "And these are plain noodles with a permanent." Everyone laughed. I felt I was among best friends, and I told them so. They thanked me for taking their children; I thanked them for saving the best children for me. I asked if I could take their picture, and they agreed. One of the staff took my camera to take a picture with me included.

Although I had more events scheduled—going to Southgate for shopping, visiting Chogyesa Temple, seeing the demarcation line between North and South Korea, attending a church service boasting a membership of over two and a half million, and going to the Korean Village—the purpose of my trip had just been fulfilled. The hours with Mr. Kim and his staff made me feel I was with my children with no miles of separation.

I missed the kids more than ever and was anxious to return home. I tried getting my flight confirmed by phone, but the concierge of the hotel advised me to go to the main building of Korean Airlines. Confidently holding my passport when I arrived at KAL, I took the elevator to the eleventh floor. I entered a room where twenty-five people worked at computers. I walked to the section labeled USA, showed the attendant my return ticket, and asked for a reservation on Sunday night's flight. The woman keyed in my information. *Now I'm getting somewhere. Wrong.* She told me that Sunday night's flight was full and that all flights out of Korea were booked until August 10, which was four days after I was scheduled to return. I attempted to keep my cool and tried another tactic.

"Can my ticket be transferred to another airline?" I asked. "Like Northwest Orient?"

She leafed through my ticket. "No, not this kind of ticket," she informed me.I began to put my papers in my purse. My defenses broke down and I cried.

"Why do you cry?" the woman asked sympathetically.

"I want to go home," I sobbed. *I'm being held prisoner; I'll never see my kids again, and I'll never get to leave for America.*

The staff frantically pressed buttons. At least five people worked on it as they looked at me between clicking. The boss assured me from time to time, "We will do our best." An hour and a half later, the boss approached me waving a paper, "OK, lady, we have confirmed your reservation." I smiled broadly and hastily showed him pictures of my children. He passed them around the office, and the staff smiled too.

My only other concern was how to transport my luggage and souvenirs, which now consisted of two brass candelabras, eight brass napkin rings, three banks, miscellaneous brass, one mahogany tea table, two cases of chopsticks, one shaman wand, a kite, and two dolls? *Maybe the shaman wand will hold the answer*. The answer was I had to purchase additional luggage. Sunday's flight went smoothly. I arrived in New York City and checked into an airport hotel. Elliot and the kids met me the next afternoon. While I was fortunate to have had the opportunity to visit South Korea, I was glad to be home.

CHAPTER 30: IS THERE ROOM AT THE INN ?

Having added three children to the family, Elliot and I were outgrowing our house. A larger house with a big yard became available on our block as part of the urban renewal movement. York City was rehabilitating two city blocks that had been abandoned after Hurricane Agnes in 1972. We were fourth on the lottery for the house. The three people on the list ahead of us opted not to buy it. The house became ours for $950, and we had to completely refurbish it from basement to attic. I was excited to watch the renovations, especially when others did the work.

I worked full-time as a school psychologist but began a part-time clinical practice under supervision. My goal was to accumulate three thousand hours, which would qualify me to take my licensing exam. Once licensed, I could begin my own practice.

One night in the fall of 1982, I had an appointment with a family who were in the process of adopting a nine-year-old Canadian

Indian boy, Sam. He had lived with them less than a week, and they were visibly distraught. He was hyperactive and already in trouble at school. They felt certain there was a history that the agency hadn't disclosed to them. His background was complicated but well-documented in a file three-inches thick. Sam had a history of trauma, of which his family had been informed.

I evaluated him to form a diagnosis. One of the techniques I employed was the family drawing test: my only directions were to draw a family. Sam drew figures from "Goldilocks and the Three Bears," and he told me a story about his drawing. His drawing and the accompanying story indicated that, to him, families were fairy tales and not real. Goldilocks (Sam) was the intruder in this family, and she (he) felt threatened by the adult bears (parents and other adults in authority). At the end of the three-hour evaluation, I diagnosed him with attention deficit hyperactivity disorder with very superior intelligence. I recommended family therapy as well as individual therapy for Sam. The family was sure there must be more.

I returned to the evaluation room to let Sam know I would be having a session with him and his family the following week. Sam seemed receptive. When we returned to the waiting room, however, Sam's parents were gone. They had told the caseworker they were sure the agency was not being honest. The parents felt they had made a mistake, and they were no longer interested in Sam. They said they'd bring his belongings to the agency in the morning.

I had just witnessed people abandoning a child. I empathized for Sam. I put my arms around him, and we both cried. I took him home with me while the agency worked on a placement. But Sam didn't go to any other placement; he became part of our family. Now we were a family of six, with all four of the kids arriving within the past two years.

CHAPTER 31: KEEPING UP APPEARANCES

In November we moved into the "new" old house. We hadn't yet painted or wallpapered it, but it was ready for a family. And we were definitely a family. The local newspaper highlighted us during National Adoption Week. I ran a preadolescent adoption group in my house for adopted children and their parents who were coping with adjustments. The group was highlighted in the paper as well. We looked great in the pictures.

When Lilly was naturalized, they took a picture of me holding her. I had written a book called *The Legend of the Bear*, which was a tale for children waiting to be adopted. The newspaper did a spread. A couple years later when Jan Lee won a poster contest, once again her picture appeared in the paper. We looked like a nice, well-adjusted family—like that family at Hershey for "sweetheart's weekend" three years before.

While I continued to see my therapist, Tom, we involved ourselves in family therapy, which usually centered on behavioral issues with Sam and Jan Lee. While my personality clashed with Jan Lee's, Elliot's clashed with Sam's. Some of Elliot's former anger with me was transferred to Sam. Disagreement about discipline methods continued.

Our house had come together nicely, and the following year we were on both a house and garden tour. The kids and I made a brick pathway along the entire side of the house using bricks we found at sites where old buildings had been destroyed. We loaded bricks in the trunk of my car, and using a wheelbarrow we'd unload them at the side of the house. We were proud of our design and the way it curved around the bay window.

On some Saturdays Elliot would pick up a family pack of chicken with the side orders, and we would eat on the patio. One Saturday Elliot had been argumentative earlier in the day, but I had learned not to say anything. Something had upset him at dinner; he crushed his paper plate of food and stormed into the house, where he remained alone the rest of the evening. On Sunday he wouldn't go to church with us; he insisted that Jan Lee didn't have to go either, but that the rest of us should go. We went.

Later that evening Jan Lee had taken a bath, but hadn't emptied her dirty water from the tub. I called her to do it so I could bathe Lilly. Jan Lee ignored me. I called her two more times. She slowly came down the steps, and when she reached the third from the bottom, I took her by the arm and said, "When I call, you are to come. There's no reason why Lilly has to take a bath in a dirty tub." Jan Lee fell forward, biting her lip as she fell. She yelled, "Dad, she hit me, she punched me, she kicked me."

Hearing Elliot charging up the stairs, I took Lil in my arms and ran out the back door of the upstairs balcony yelling that I hadn't done anything. As I ran, he was telling Jan Lee to call Children's Services Agency.

I panicked as I went to a neighbor's house. What he said triggered a memory I couldn't get under control. It had taken me back to my childhood when the social workers came and took all of us away. I kept repeating to Mary, my neighbor, "They're going to take my kids away; they're going to take all of them." I was hyperventilating and asked Mary for a phone book. I located my therapist's home number and called him. He talked me out of my panic and convinced me that the scenario would not happen. Benjamin came over to see if I was OK. He had seen and heard everything that occurred.

Then Sam came to Mary's door. He had been emptying trash for the next day's collection and found a pornographic magazine. One of the articles was "Teaching Your Teenage Daughter to Give Head." I heaved at the thought and tried to dismiss it from my mind, staying focused on the present incident. The boys were concerned for me, and we stayed at Mary's that night.

The next day Children's Services visited Jan Lee at school to interview her. Her school was one of the ones where I was the school psychologist. Later that day they called me to ask if it would be safe for her to come home. *How dare them!* I thought. *How could they think of accusing me of abuse?* Overlapping that thought was a deeper voice that reminded me to whom I was talking. It distinctly told me to keep my voice under control, reminding me of the horror stories I had heard about people who show negative emotions to social workers. I calmly asked why there would be a question about her being safe since she has always been safe at home.

"Well, there was the incident last night, you know," came her terse reply as only a young social worker who has never been married and has never raised children can intonate.

"Yes, she will continue to be safe," I said. I was not going to accept their bait. It seemed to take forever, but the letter arrived in the mail stating that the reported accusations were unfounded. The incident kept me more on guard than ever before with both Jan Lee and Elliot. There was no doubt about it—they were working as a team.

My physical affection for Elliot had been waning, and now I wanted no part of him. I lay awake at night at the farthest possible distance from him pretending to be asleep. I lay on my side with my back to him, scrunched up against the frame of the octagonal waterbed. Before going to bed, I would make sure the upstairs balcony door was unlocked just in case I needed to exit quickly. After he was asleep and snoring, I would go to the family room, sit in the corner of the couch, and wonder how we ever got to this place. This was never the picture I had in mind for a family. The "Kodak moments" were severely out of focus.

CHAPTER 32: GIVE ME SHELTER

Another Sunday night Elliot had been drinking both beer and whisky, a combination that was a red flag in terms of Elliot's physical aggression. An argument started—I don't even know over what; and somehow I ended up on the clay-colored, ceramic-tiled kitchen floor up against the wall with Elliot kicking the hell out of me. I saw the tip of his brown boot come at my face, and then I felt the blow and repeatedly yelled, "STOP!" I put my arms over my head to protect my face and head. Benjamin and Jan Lee ran down the stairs.

"Dad, STOP!" yelled Ben.

"Dad, STOP! You're hurting her," yelled Jan Lee.

Elliot hastily left the kitchen. I got up hurting and crying and called 911. The police came, took one look at me, and took all the kids and me to the shelter for battered women. On the way to the shelter, the officer informed us that I was not the first woman who had called about physical violence at the hands of Elliot. This was news to me. The kids and I spent the night huddled together in a room.

When everyone was awake the next morning, Benjamin and Sam were very quiet and sad. Jan Lee was perky and walked off to school from the shelter before we even knew she was gone. Sam and Benjamin got a ride to school, and Lil stayed with me. I was embarrassed when I talked to the shelter counselor in the morning. They advised me to press charges and get a protection from abuse order (PFA). I told them that I couldn't, that Elliot was an attorney, and we were a professional family in the community. I told them Elliot's license was recently reinstated and I couldn't do this to him. I felt shame for Elliot's actions. They told me I was not the only attorney's wife to grace their doors, that abuse is not owned by any class in particular, and that I would be surprised to know who had come for shelter. I thought they were telling me this to ease my mind. I had never heard any of this before. I attached this sort of behavior to my biological family. They also told me that I was not doing anything to Elliot and that he had done this—not me. They invited me to attend their support group that met every Wednesday night. I said, "I'll talk to an attorney about a PFA order."

They suggested I undergo a physical examination I had bruises on my face, left arm, and hip, and my nose appeared to be broken. I walked the several blocks back to my house, and from there I drove to my doctor's office. I decided on the way that I was too embarrassed to tell him what had happened. The doctor was also a family friend and would think badly of Elliot. I also felt there might have been something I could have done to prevent the abuse but didn't do. *The only bruises that show are on my face*, I thought. I saw one on my arm, however, so I rolled my sleeves down. When I saw my doctor, I told him how I had run smack into the edge of an open door.

"During the night," I said, "Lilly had cried out, and I jumped up in the dark, not realizing the door was open, and I went full force when I hit the door." (This had actually happened to me as a kid. I remember my nose hurting and going to my parents' room to tell them. But my father told me to go back to bed and tell him in the morning.) I knew this injury would be compatible with my story. I was convincing, and I joked about how clumsy I was. My nose was broken. (A year or so later when I told the doctor the truth, he felt bad that I had protected Elliot and his brutality.)

I went to an attorney who explained what was involved in a PFA order. I told him to draw up the papers and give them to me so I could think it over. When Elliot came home later, he acted as if nothing had happened: no apology, no asking about the kids, nothing. I put the papers on the bathroom counter that night with a note saying I would not file them if he agreed to go to counseling with me. He agreed, and I tore up the papers. Something changed as a result of seeing the papers. He knew that Access (the name of the shelter) had been involved. He knew that another attorney knew what he had done. He did not physically abuse me after that; however, he chose another form of abuse that does not leave physical marks.

CHAPTER 33: CAN THIS MARRIAGE BE SAVED ?

True to his word, Elliot went to counseling with me. He sat there—he attended. No one would be able to accuse him of not being cooperative. Beyond attending, he did nothing. I thought: *maybe I can change this man by pressuring him to go to counseling. Once there he will see what he has done wrong and, once knowing, of course he'll be a caring, compassionate man.* Between counseling sessions, I suggested we try the assignments in order to learn to communicate more effectively. We needed to use "I messages" such as, "When you yell at me, I feel afraid, and I need for you not to yell." There was no practice between sessions. I began to use the sessions to express my anger toward him over the abuse. I yelled at him while he passively sat there and responded in a soft voice. He tried to make me look like the aggressor. Tom, my therapist, saw through Elliot, who was not aware that he was exposed. It was the first time I felt safe. It brought about a voice in me that I never knew I had. I caught an occasional "what a bitch" glance from the other clients in the waiting room as we exited—me red-faced and tense with Elliot playing the "poor me" role.

With all the time spent as parents and professionals, Elliot and I did not do much socializing. Occasionally on weekends during the summer we would visit a couple with whom we had become friends. They had an adopted child who was in my preadolescent adoption group. I liked Matilda's offbeat personality, and I saw her as intelligent and creative. Her husband, Frank, appeared intelligent but tense. Their house was by the river, and we'd go out on their pontoon boat, eat hard-shelled crabs, and drink beer. The kids played in the woods and in the water while we played Trivial Pursuit. We were four intelligent people kicking back on the hot weekends.

Other adults from the adoption group brought it to my attention in the fall that, while I was having group with the kids, Matilda was hanging all over Elliot. I'd seen her hanging all over other men, however; so I dismissed it as part of her personality. I noticed that when we were at the river, Elliot and Matilda frequently groped one another while slow dancing. I listened to the song lyrics, "Every time you go away, you take a piece of me with you." I thought: *It probably feels comfortable for Elliot to dance with someone as tall as he is. He doesn't have to bend down—like he has to do with me—for her to touch his shoulders.* She slid her hand over the front of his pants, and I got the feeling it wasn't just the beer and slow music. When I confronted Elliot about this, he said I was "making a mountain out of a molehill."

In January of the next year, I found a note card in Elliot's brown leather jacket signed by Matilda. When I asked him about it, he said it was just a friendship card. I didn't think so. One day when Matilda called him, I listened. She was crying and telling him how much it hurt her when he had to leave and couldn't stay with her.

What is it that compels us to ignore facets of reality that we find unpleasant ? I actually asked him for an explanation, and he made up something lame. I wanted to believe it. I still wanted to believe that we could make a go of the marriage even if it was only for the kids' sake. I wanted them to grow up with a mother and a father; for less than that to happen would mean I had failed. My purpose in adopting was to provide a family for the kids and raise them to have opportunities for connection (and in so doing have a connection myself). I wanted to convert Sam's "Goldilocks and the Three Bears" picture into a real live family—one made up of human beings he could call *mom*, *dad*, *brother*, and *sister*—in which he had a place. I kept this picture active in my mind.

On a Tuesday evening in February, I found a gray sweater in a gift box on the floor of our bedroom closet. It was a sweater for an adult male. The dark gray wool was dotted with very small maroon hearts. On the card was an Oscar Wilde quote about "wanting only the best," and was signed by Matilda. Elliot still denied the relationship. He said he'd never seen the sweater and had no idea where it came from.

At 7:30 a.m. on Ash Wednesday, the phone rang. "It's Matilda," she said to me. "Elliot tells me you think we're having an affair. Well, we are." The words hurt. The vision hurt more. I saw the picture of a family dissolving before my eyes, as if caustic bleach had spilled over it making it disappear. First, the color faded; then the figures appeared as blobs, and finally the entire picture was no more. I yelled, "NO!" I hung up the phone, raced to the bedroom, and told Elliot what Matilda had said. He said nothing and continued getting dressed. I cried and yelled, demanding to know if it was true. Benjamin and Sam appeared at the door, alarmed by what I was saying. They felt my pain as well as their own. The three of us sat at the kitchen table not wanting to believe it, but at the same time we knew it was true. Jan Lee, like Elliot, continued to get dressed and went off to school. Elliot walked into the kitchen and asked why the boys hadn't left for school.

"Their whole world has just crumbled, and you want to know why they're not at school? How dare you expect them to go!" I screamed at him. Elliot went to work, and the rest of that day was a blur.

That evening Jan Lee announced, "Well, Mom, Dad says you two are breaking up, and I have to decide where I want to be. I'm going to White Street with Dad. Bye."

"Good—go!" I said, as she ran down the stairs.

White Street? What's on White Street? I wondered. As it turned out, Elliot had an apartment on White Street where he and Matilda rendezvoused regularly. Jan Lee had known this for quite some time.

She talked about it at school, and other kids had asked Sam about it. Since Sam didn't know about the apartment, he shrugged it off as attention-getting behavior on Jan Lee's part, and he didn't mention it to me.

The next day I emptied all her drawers, cleared out her closet, put everything in bags, and gave it all to a family who had eight adopted children. Elliot later went to that family to get the clothing back. I don't think they were happy about it, but they did hand it over. While he was gone, I gathered his stuff and put it in the living room. There had been a picture of us framed in a ceramic heart magnet on the refrigerator; I tore him out of the picture. Later, Lilly pointed out the picture to a visitor at the house and said, "Look, my daddy's not here anymore."

Sam expressed guilt for not telling me about the time he saw Elliot and Matilda go into our bedroom and later saw Elliot come out with his belt unbuckled. He thought that if he had told me, then maybe this would not have happened. I assured him it had nothing to do with him. Sam was angry when he saw Elliot the next time.

"Why did you have to go and sleep with another woman?" he shouted from the other side of the room.

"Why wasn't your mother sleeping with me?" Elliott instantly shot back.

For an instant a wave of guilt shot through me as if now I was to blame for his behavior. I wasn't buying it.

"Get out of here," I yelled. "How dare you to try to turn this around on me." As soon as he left, I called a locksmith and had the locks changed—something I heard Elliot recommend to his divorce clients. He and Matilda both thought it would be nice if we all just got along. She wasn't even drunk when she expressed this.

I saw my family doctor and told him what was going on. I was not sleeping well, felt helpless, and was an emotional wreck. He told me that it's very difficult to go through a divorce and that I had many complications. He recommended that I stay in therapy even though Elliot was no longer attending. He prescribed an antidepressant and a sleeping aid, which up until that time I had felt were only for "weak" people. The antidepressant took about three weeks to become effective, but then my energy restored and my sleeping improved. I realized for the first time in my life that it is a position of strength to be able to ask for help.

In November, Elliot apologized that he had moved out and had the affair. He said it was over with Matilda, and he moved back in. I believed the separation had been positive, and he realized what he had abandoned. We spent the holidays together. He was more generous than ever with gifts. He gave me a leather coat, in addition to an emerald and diamond gold band. This was quite a contrast to the year before when he gave me a tire iron and other things for my car in case I was stuck in an emergency on the highway. It's amazing what nice gifts guilt can produce. I was happy. Later in the day, the boys and Lilly were playing with their toys, and Elliot was listening to his new portable CD player with earphones. Jan Lee was hanging out with me, which was unusual.

"Mom," she said, "I have a secret to share with you." I felt a twinge of warm feeling for her. I imagined: *Maybe she missed being part of a family while she and Elliot were gone.* I thought. *She's really trying now.*

"Mom, Dad's still sleeping with Matilda. I thought you might want to know," she said.

"You're lying! Jan Lee, you can't take being part of this family," I said. I held her arm, and walked her to the family room and motioned for Elliot to remove his earphones.

"Jan Lee just confided in me that you are still sleeping with Matilda. I think I know her motivation."

"She's trying to stir up trouble," he said looking at us. "Jan Lee! Go to your room." I smiled at Jan Lee as she stalked up the stairs. *Finally, he has her number. That's progress.*

We all existed together. Once he was back, it was Elliot who did not want physical intimacy, which made me wonder whether he was depressed about the events. I had planned to take a sabbatical from the LIU the next school year and transition into a full-time practice while I took clinical courses at Johns Hopkins. My practice was growing with referrals from the adoption agency as well as from the medical doctors where I rented an office. Another school psychologist, Dan, joined me, and we became the most perfect business partners for a long time after. I was also preparing to take my licensing exam so I could go into a full-time clinical practice of my own.

One Saturday morning in April, I went to my office and Elliot went to his. Something was wrong with my car; so I called him at his office but didn't reach him. After I saw a couple clients, I called him again. A man whose voice I didn't recognize answered. I told him my name, and the man explained that Elliot and Matilda had just left for lunch."

I immediately felt nauseated. I told my next client I had an emergency and could not see him. It became obvious that he and Matilda had never stopped their affair. I felt guilty because I had not believed Jan Lee and had insisted she was wrong. She had been telling the truth, however, regardless of her motivation. I went to his office. I hoped to catch them together when they returned, but at the same time I didn't want to catch them. Maybe if I didn't catch them, Elliot would have a reasonable explanation. I went to his office, but no one returned. The man who answered the phone had gone to the deli. He had taped a message to Elliot's door that read, "Julie called—I told her you and Matilda left for lunch. She wants you to call her." Elliot didn't come home that night, but he came to the house the next day, April 15, with the income tax return that needed to be signed by me.

It became clear that getting back together was a ruse to keep me in a receptive mood since it would be to his advantage if we filed jointly. Nothing had changed. Previously we had driven to Maryland to get married on December 29, even though invitations stated January 28, because being married presented a tax break. He had played me for the fool once again. I signed and he left for the last time.

CHAPTER 34: A PAUSE IN THE DAY'S OCCUPATION

A certain peace settled into the house. Benjamin, Sam, Lilly, and I did quite well together. Sam, being the hyperactive kid he was, would get loud and argumentative on occasion, but he was manageable. He also responded to correction as long as he was on medication. I didn't realize how much tension there had been with our different parenting styles. It felt liberating not to have my authority undermined.

We settled into a new schedule. My office was within two blocks of the house; so after school the kids would come to the office. Lilly enjoyed reuniting with me after a school day and then playing with toys or drawing pictures, displaying her artistic talent. Sam and Ben did their homework in an adjoining room. The office staff was supportive. We were healing.

The kids went to Elliot's every other weekend. The first few weekends were hard, especially for Lil. She broke my heart each time because she wanted to stay with me.

"Mom, I don't want to go to Dad's," she'd plead as she stood on the top step. "I want to stay with you."

"Lil, you have to go; there's nothing I can do about it," I told her. I'd silently cuss Elliot out all over again for creating this mess. What I didn't tell her was that, if a parent obstructs visitation, he or she can be held in contempt of court, be put in jail, and not be available to the child at all. Ben interceded and reassured Lilly, taking her hand and gently leading her down the steps.

One weekend in July, only Ben and Lilly returned. Sam had decided to remain with Elliot. That hurt, especially because it occurred so suddenly. What I didn't know was that Elliot was putting pressure on all of them to live with him so he would be able to reclaim the house for himself, the kids, and Matilda. His grand scheme was that I'd be out on the street and not able to afford to keep the house. He began by allowing the kids to do whatever they wanted when they were with him. There were no routines to follow or chores to do, and they could eat whatever they wanted. Sam was allowed to skateboard down the middle of a two-way street. And Elliot didn't require Sam to take his medication. He let Sam think his problem was with me. As far as he was concerned, Sam was not hyperactive, and my diagnosis—as well as the diagnoses of three medical doctors—did not exist. Sam was vulnerable.

Benjamin and Lilly didn't take the bait. While both of them had a good relationship with Elliot and loved him and knew he loved them, they also knew where they felt secure. One weekend when Elliot had taken them to New Jersey to visit with friends and Matilda's relatives, Ben was upset because he didn't like the idea that Elliot was trying to replace me with Matilda. The older kids stayed up to watch sci-fi movies, and Elliot and Matilda had taken Lilly to bed with them. Lilly wanted to be with me, which made Elliot angry. When Benjamin heard Elliot's raised voice, he brought Lil to be with him and the older kids. Also, he heard Elliot tell Matilda's mother that I approved of their relationship.

Later that summer Lilly, Benjamin, and I spent a week at the shore with friends. Everyone told me I needed to get away, and the trip was long overdue. Friends of mine looked after the house for us. The day before I was due to return, my friends watching the house called and said that Elliot had come to the house and taken much of the furnishings and belongings. I returned to a half-empty house. I immediately called the police and filed a description of everything that had been taken: the dining room table and chairs, the washer, the dryer, the TV, the stereo, and miscellaneous items—even Benjamin's paper-route money. Also missing was an oil portrait of Lilly painted by a friend of mine; oriental rugs, which I had inherited from my parents ; and my mother's diamond dinner ring, which I inherited from my mother, were also taken.

The police could do nothing but take the report. They said that it was Elliot's house too. "I had the locks changed," I told them. But they said that didn't matter because legally you can't break into your own house. Apparently, while Benjamin was visiting over a weekend, Elliot had stolen Benjamin's key for the new lock and had planned to enter while we were on vacation.

The neighbors saw Elliot, Matilda, Jan Lee, and Sam removing things but didn't realize that they were taking them deceitfully. Since they had heard no forceful entry, they assumed this had been prearranged between Elliot and me.

My brother Ivan drove down to help me recover the stolen items. I especially wanted the oil painting of Lilly, my mother's ring, and the oriental rugs. I took Lilly and my brother with me over to Elliot's apartment. It seemed as though no one was home; so I broke a windowpane in the door to enter. As I was leaving, Elliot and Matilda drove up and called the police. Two officers arrived.

"Put down the things in your arms," they commanded.

"But these things are mine," I said. "They were taken out of my house while I was away, and I was just reclaiming them."

"Lady, put down the things," the police officer said sternly. A second officer stepped out of his car.

"Earlier in the day these items were reported stolen," he said. The police were about to let things rest when Elliot informed them that I had outstanding parking tickets. They checked and found out that I did. They put handcuffs on me and told me to sit in the back of their car.

"Don't feel sorry for Mom, Lil. She did this to herself," Jan Lee said to a sobbing Lilly.

"Everything is fine Lilly, Elliott responded.

"I want to stay with Uncle Ivan," Lilly said. She took his hand, and the two of them walked back to the house.

The police interrogated me in the back of their car. I gave outlandish answers to everything they asked. They asked how old I was, and I said eighty-four. They asked how tall I was, and I said six eight. They asked my date of birth, and I told them February 30, 1918. When they asked my occupation, I told the truth and said I was a psychologist. The officer said, "Sure you're a psychologist" and sneered at me.

They took me to the duty magistrate's office, and I had to pay my parking tickets before they released me. I walked home where Lilly, Ivan, and Benjamin were waiting and glad to see me. Three years later, through the courts, the oriental rugs were returned to me. Elliot was also ordered to return my mother's ring, but he denied taking it, and the diamond dinner ring was never returned to me. To this day I don't know if Lilly's portrait exists.

A couple days later, I received a call at my office and I recognized the arresting police officer's voice. He asked if there was a psychologist named Julie working there.

"Yes, there is, officer," I said.

"Oh," he responded and hung up.

The next Friday evening, I took the kids to a local restaurant where they offered three tacos for a dollar with all the trimmings. We had taken the kids there a number of times before, and they enjoyed it. As we walked into the establishment, I saw Elliot, Matilda, her daughter Dorothea, Sam, and Jan Lee sitting at a table in the middle of the room. I saw red and almost backed away, but a voice told me *I have as much right to be here*. Ben was hesitant and suggested we go home.

"No," I said firmly, "We're here for tacos. And Elliot and Matilda don't own the First Cap." The only table left was by the front window, which was directly in front of them. We had our dinner, and I talked to Dorothea when she came over to see Lilly. *OK, I can handle this.* A couple of times I felt hot tears roll down my cheeks, but I quickly wiped them away. I was doing great. I just needed to continue to reassure myself. When they prepared to leave, I immediately rose to my feet, looked at Elliot, and yelled, "All this for a goddamn piece of ass. I sure hope it was worth it." I was as surprised at what came out of my mouth as the other customers; my dentist was among the diners.

As Elliot and Matilda slunk out the door, the waitress came to my table and told me to calm down. I gave her a condensed version of what was happening. She said she understood, but that I should remember that there were children present. We finished our tacos and left. I must admit that as sorry as I was to have said that in front of the kids, I felt as though a load had been lifted from me. I was making progress.

CHAPTER 35: THE HIGH PRICE OF PROGRESS

Elliot filed an emergency relief petition, and the York County Courts served me papers on Monday. Elliot asked the courts to place Lilly and Ben in his custody because of my "mental condition" as evidenced by my public outburst on Friday night. The judge saw no emergency and viewed my reaction as a result of circumstances that Elliot had created for himself. Elliot then filed a petition for custody, and the judge ordered a psychological evaluation to include the entire family with recommendations for custody and visitation. The judge also ordered family sessions so that the evaluator could assess the family dynamics. A couple of the sessions were intense.

Before this stage of the divorce, Elliot had never consented to family therapy. Now, in this time of crisis, a psychologist was trying to work with the entire family in the same room. Elliot, Jan Lee, and Sam had planned ahead. Elliot appeared passive and calm; Sam sat next to him cracking his gum; Jan Lee sat on the other side of Elliot, occasionally smirking at me. For as much as I was trying to keep my emotions under control, this would probably be the only opportunity for me to tell them all what I thought. And so I vented my anger. The frustrated psychologist admonished me for playing into their hands. I angrily asked him if he had ever gone through divorce and custody. I apparently hit a chord since he bellowed, “My personal life is none of your business. You’re crossing boundaries.”

After the third session, the psychologist knew it was futile to try to repair the relationship. In his final report to the court, he criticized me for reacting emotionally, but conceded that Elliot had formed an alliance with Sam and Jan Lee and purposely set me up to react. He concluded that Lilly and Benjamin’s personalities were more like mine, and that to remove them would only create more volatility in the situation. Thus he recommended they stay with me while Sam and Jan Lee visit me every other weekend.

Jan Lee would have none of this; and when I went to pick her up, she wasn’t at Elliot’s apartment. I wasn’t going to force the issue. There was nothing to gain from her visits, and I was sure she would be a disruptive influence on us. Sam also resisted, but I thought it might work out if he visited without Elliot's influence. Benjamin thought Sam was too embarrassed to visit after the way he behaved at the family sessions. I tried a couple of sessions with Sam in therapy, but he was uncooperative and mimicked me. The psychologist recommended I let Sam know that I wasn't moving anywhere and that when he was ready, he could come to me. That ended some of the game playing.

Elliot, however, didn't stop the custody action with the psychological recommendation and pressed for a full custody trial. Since all the local judges knew Elliot and me, the hearing was delayed. January brought snow, ice, and the custody hearing. Judge Winthrop, a retired judge from Lancaster County, would hear the case. I did my homework. I called the abuse shelter, asked them to confirm the date and reason we had spent the night, and asked if they would testify. My character witnesses included my closest neighbor, who knew parts of the conflict; Dr. Jim, our family doctor; and one of the doctors in whose office I rented space. Connie, our caseworker from the adoption agency, also testified about the relationship she saw between Benjamin, Lilly, and me. The psychologist who had performed the court-ordered custody evaluation also testified that. in his professional opinion, the separation from me would have negative effects on Ben and Lil.

Elliot did not focus on what the kids needed and wanted. He used the tactic demeaning my character, stating that Jan Lee and Sam didn't want to live with me. What Elliot did not know was that I had some love letters in my possession that were from his star witness, Agatha, who was head of the adoption agency.

The previous year I needed a copy of our tax return, which he always completed. I had asked him several times for a copy, but he never gave it to me. One afternoon he was out of town, I stopped at his office and told the secretary I needed to get a copy of the returns. She unlocked the door to his office and returned to her desk, leaving me to look for the returns.

I wasn't prepared for what I found. After looking in his filing cabinet and finding nothing, I opened the bottom right-hand drawer of his desk. I found a bottle of Jim Beam and some porno magazines. That was true to character. Finally, I found the tax return in his right-hand top drawer. But something made me keep looking although I had no idea for what.

In his middle drawer were many cards and letters from women and a very hurtful letter to him from Jan Lee. There were also love notes from Matilda expressing how cozy she felt when she looked across the room and saw his socks on the floor, how she so loved the bath he had given her, and how the sex was so fulfilling. I continued to read. There was also a letter from me dated over a year ago expressing how hopeful I was that we could all be a family again.

There were several long letters from Agatha, his star witness. She had sent him plans for building an A-frame house on our property at Lake Meade. She expressed her sorrow that he was going through this hell with me, letting him know she was always there for him. One letter described how she felt when she saw his blue eyes looking at her from across the courtroom and how holding his hand under the table at lunch made her feel, and other comments of a similar nature.

I felt a knife go through me. Agatha was head of the adoption agency, and I looked upon her as a mother figure. I had taught some of her kids in gifted classes, shared my life story with her, and let her read my writings and poetry regarding adoption. She had asked me as a psychologist to form and run the preteen adoption group.

In addition she had helped Elliot. She single-handedly spearheaded his career back into practice after his five-year suspension from the bar, referring all her adoption cases to him. If it were not for her, he would have had a very difficult time rebuilding a practice. Here, however, in her handwriting were pages and pages of love letters. I was unaware of this relationship.

Then there was the letter from Jan Lee, written during those few months when we were back together:

> Dear Dad,
>
> If you don't divorce Mom, you'll lose me. Elvira loves you, Matilda loves you, Agatha loves you, and I love you. And what do you do? You go back to Mom. She doesn't love you; she hurts you. Think of it, Dad—you'll lose all of us if you stay with her. You have to make a choice—is it going to be her or us?
>
> Love, your daughter,
>
> Jan Lee

The hot tears rolled down my cheeks. This one drawer contained years and years of deceit and a mountain of pain. My mother figure, my friend, and my daughter had all betrayed me. I sobbed. The drawer contained adoration of him from all these women. This drawer was obviously where he stored his ego.

I looked around the room at the pictures of the kids he had on the wall. They were all there, both from his first marriage and mine. He looked like the poster child for the happy little family campaign. I felt nauseated. He was such a hypocrite. I dried my tears, took a few good deep breaths, and breezed through the outer office. I thanked his secretary and let her know I found what I was looking for.

I left with the tax return and much more. Within the pages of the tax return were some of the letters and cards. I hadn't taken them all. I left some scattered as they had been in the drawer, but I had a representative sample—certainly enough to pass on to my attorney and certainly enough to make me smile as Agatha took the stand in the courtroom that January morning.

His attorney began with questions about Elliot's character, for which she praised him. She told how she came to know him, what a wonderful father he was, and how attached the children were to him. The lawyer led her into an introduction of herself and qualified her as a national expert in the field of adoption.

Along with praising Elliot, Agatha also questioned my capacity to be a good parent, citing my relationship with Jan Lee. Then Elliot's lawyer produced my autobiography, which I had previously written for the adoption home study. I had put my heart and soul into those pages, and now they were being used against me. I gave those words to someone I thought I could trust as a prerequisite to adoption. My childhood was cited, as well as my relationship with my mother and how I felt about her when she said, "You can't make a silk purse out of a sow's ear." Agatha questioned whether someone with my background could be a good parent, suggesting I might duplicate the way I was raised. I saw the judge taking notes during her expert testimony. Then it was my lawyer's turn to question the witness.

J. Christian Ness, my attorney, reiterated Agatha's credentials and admitted that she was recognized nationally in the field of adoption. He pumped up her professional reputation to Elliot's satisfaction and his attorney. Then he quietly walked back to the table, rifled through some papers and approached the witness stand.

"Good morning, Ms. Gibbons," he began. "I want you to listen to some correspondence and ask if the writer is you." "When I see your blue eyes across the court room at an adoption hearing, my heart goes a flutter, Love, Aggie." Before he gave her time to answer, he read another card, "when we are holding hands under the table at lunch———-" and another, each time emphasizing the signature, "Love, Aggie."

"Judge," she said with a red face and an alarmed voice, "please stop him from reading any more. These notes were personal."

"I agree that these letters and cards were very personal," my attorney said, in a loud voice echoing in the courtroom, glaring straight into Agatha's eyes. "You must take some personal responsibility for the breakup of this family!" Needless to say, the judge dismissed her as an expert witness on the grounds that the letters constituted a conflict of interest in testifying against me.

Elliot's next witness was Elvira, who was a supervisor at Children's Services. She and Elliot had known each other for years.

She was sworn in and her credentials as an expert witness were presented and accepted. Elvira extolled Elliot's good character over the time she had known him. She knew him to be a fine example of fatherhood from his first family as well. She talked about a time when Jan Lee stayed at her house for two weeks providing Jan Lee and us a break from each other. She said that, in all her years as a children's caseworker, she had never seen a child more frightened of her mother than Jan Lee was of me.

"Was there any more to your relationship to Elliot," my attorney asked Elvira.

"I don't know what you're implying." she responded.

"You have established in this court room, that you know him quite well," he continued. "But how well do you know his wife ? Have you ever visited the house while she was there? Have you ever seen her exercising her parental skills? Have you ever done anything socially that involved you, Elliot, and her? "

"No," Elvira answered to all of these questions.

My attorney returned to the table and sat down. Then the judge looked at Elvira, who was seated in the witness chair.

"While you have never seen a child who was as frightened of her mother, have you ever dealt with a child who had found her mother hanging in a closet, like Jan Lee did when she was eight years old?"

"No," she answered.

"Then you weren't even aware of Jan Lee's background," he said. "I have no further questions; you may step down." *Thank God he understands*, I thought. In my testimony I discussed the background of each of the children upon adoption and their activities since then. Finally, he talked privately with the kids, and they said they wanted to live with me. The judge dismissed us for the day saying he'd have a decision by morning.

I didn't sleep that night, but I did feel confident. The next morning the judge awarded me custody of the kids. I started to cry when he lectured Elliot and me about adopting children and not staying together, saying we each owned a part of this. He also mentioned that he knows something about adoption since he was an adoptive parent himself. Some of my tears were those of joy and relief, but some were out of shame because I didn't keep the family together.

I knew Jan Lee and Sam were merely pawns used by Elliot. I did not blame them for anything that happened but I promised myself that Ben, Lil, and I would be a family. I had amended my definition of a family.

CHAPTER 36: BLISS

Ben, Lil, and I enjoyed a period of stability and peace. Sam showed up every now and then, but Jan Lee never came to the house again. When Sam visited he'd tell me of conflicts between Elliot and Matilda. I believe he just wanted a reaction. The third time he reported a conflict I let him know that this was visitation time with him, and I didn't need Matilda and Elliot visiting through him while he was there. Once he got the idea, he respected it. I went on with my life as a single mother, and it felt good.

I'd been active in the Parent Teachers Association while the kids were in elementary school. Continuing my interest in the school system, I campaigned for a seat on the local school board. In York a school director is an elected official. I won in the primary, and my name went on the ballot for the general election. I took part in some events involving candidates where I had to speak to the audience. I was extremely self-conscious, and I didn't like this arena. Sitting around a table talking with people, working one-on-one, or working with a family was one thing, but "performing" in front of the public was another. Sometimes I'd lose my voice, and frequently my skin would break out in blotches. In spite of my anxiety, I won, which helped my self-confidence tremendously.

My life felt balanced for the first time in years. When I worked in the evening, Benjamin would see that he and Lil had dinner. Both were intelligent and motivated to learn, so homework was never an issue. I encouraged them to take part in activities they enjoyed. Ben played baseball and sang in the school chorus. He also won the Daughters of the American Revolution history award. He liked to compete but liked winning better. Lil took piano lessons, and at one time or another, she took lessons in ballet, gymnastics, swimming, and ice-skating. She played the violin, later the flute, and eventually the glockenspiel. Sometimes I'd come home from the office and find her in my bedroom trying on my dresses, shoes, and jewelry. I realized this was how she kept me with her while I was working. The first year after the divorce, I knew that the holidays would be different with so few people, but I also knew that I didn't want Benjamin and Lil to miss out on anything because of the divorce. My brother Ivan always came down for the holidays and sometimes spent several days with us providing mirth. That first Christmas I started a new tradition. While I was out shopping, I also bought myself things that I wanted, and I wrapped them as gifts from "me" to "me."

We continued with Easter egg hunts, fireworks on July 4, picnics in the summer, and traditional Thanksgivings. We played board games and cards, and I taught Ben and Lil how to play pinochle. Ivan taught them poker and blackjack, and we all enjoyed Monopoly and Scrabble. I took them to Disney World and enjoyed my leisure time. We took several trips to Cancun where Lil said, that she was happier than ever before. They were great travelers sporting their backpacks and scurrying through airports.

They didn't have the typical sibling relationship. Ben was good at cajoling Lil when he wanted to do one thing and she another. Lil was also good at getting her way—not by being demanding, but because Ben and I adored her. I spent more quality time with them as a single parent than they ever had with two parents who were so conflicted. My dream of a family was fulfilled.

In 1989 I received a call from a psychiatrist friend of mine asking if I would take Wesley, a sixteen-year-old, for temporary emergency placement while they found a new adoptive family. I questioned "temporary" and had assurances that it was short-term. Wesley was from Korea, and he got along well with Benjamin, Lilly, and me. He liked everything to be organized and clean, and he readily pitched in to help. I received a call from the psychiatrist who told me that the potential family placement had fallen through, but they had other families to interview. Over time it became apparent that there were no other families, and Wesley stayed. I adopted him after he was eighteen, and he, like his siblings, was naturalized as an American citizen.

CHAPTER 37: LUCK

That was it. I'd had it with men taking advantage of me. I went back to my peaceful coexistence. My life revolved around work, home, and the school board.

I was very tired at the end of a day. I'd had a history of sleep problems since I was two, and the marriage to Elliot hadn't helped since I felt I needed to be on guard during the night. But now I was having more trouble getting to sleep and staying asleep. When I got home, I'd drink a beer or two and talk with Ben and Lil. And after they went to bed, I'd have another beer and take one with me while I watched TV in bed. Sometimes I'd fall asleep with the can still in my hand, and when I woke up in the middle of the night, the bed sheets would be wet and smell like beer. I'd get up, change the sheets, and have another beer. In the morning I'd be up with the kids, see them off to school, and go back to sleep for a couple hours before going to work. The same process repeated itself day after day. But I never missed work or the kids' activities or any meetings. I'd wait until I got home at night to pop the first beer.

My friend Shelly thought I should socialize more and possibly meet someone to date. He talked me into joining a service club that also had a social component. The meetings usually took place once a month at a local restaurant. We'd meet at the bar, have a couple of beers before the meeting, and then stop at the bar before going home.

One Monday night I met Steve, who was a member. He was tan and had white hair, an angular face, and steel-blue eyes framed by silver-rimmed glasses. He asked some intelligent questions, and I talked with him at the bar after the meeting. Steve was well-spoken and intelligent, and he had a sense of humor. He had another trait in common with me: he liked beer and was very proud of his capacity. He wasn't divorced, but he told me that his wife had left some time ago and maintained her own apartment. He was a good conversationalist and had many stories to tell about himself, and I was a good listener. The next time we saw each other was at a Monte Carlo night held at the river to benefit the service club.

I was directing parking when Steve came over and showed me how the parking should be arranged. Actually, he came over to flirt with me. We played the games of chance and danced that night. He was a good dancer, but I was not so good since I hadn't danced in years. Steve put my feet on his—as my dad had done many years before—and the fun we had more than made up for my lack of rhythm. It was the beginning of our relationship. The next day he sent me three dozen long-stem red roses. I had never received flowers from anyone other than my kids or my brother. I was truly flattered and felt special.

It turned out that Steve's lifestyle was much more complicated than he had first presented. Occasionally he dropped by my house. He worked in York but lived fifteen miles away. On nights when I wasn't working, he'd come over for dinner; on nights when I did work, we spoke on the phone.

After a few weeks, he told me he had a daughter born out of wedlock, which was one of the reasons his wife had left him. Up until now he had not been involved in raising his daughter, Katrina. Her mother was a drug addict and was having a difficult time raising seven-year-old Katrina along with her two older brothers and one younger sister. She neglected the kids, and I suggested he bring Katrina over to meet us, especially Lilly who was ten at the time. He brought her over one afternoon. Katrina, who looked a lot like Steve, was slender with blond hair and blue eyes; she had his bone structure and was precious. We got along well from the beginning. I took her for a walk in my garden and identified different flowers for her before Steve took her home.

A couple days later, Steve received a phone call at work from Children's Services; saying Katrina's mother had gone to a bar and had not returned. Katrina was tired of waiting for her; so she put her two-year-old sister, Jane, into the stroller and started down the stairs of their second-floor apartment. She slipped, and the two of them tumbled down the stairs. A neighbor called the police and an ambulance. Fortunately the injuries were not life threatening; Katrina had cut her lip and Jane had bumps and bruises. When the police found out the two girls had been left alone and that their mother was at a bar, they put the girls into protective custody and called Steve.

Steve couldn't take Katrina home in case his wife came back to the house. He knew she would not welcome her. I suggested he bring her to my house until we find out what was happening. Because they were unable to locate Jane's father, she remained at Children's Services. Katrina thought she was Jane's caretaker and was responsible for the fall. She missed her sister, and Jane ended up coming over until Jane's father could make other arrangements.

Initially, Lilly liked Katrina and empathized for her. I too felt compassionate. It was clear that Katrina could not go back home until her mother received help and stabilized her life. Her mother promised to try. She had tried to stop in the past; she had been in several rehabs but always returned to drugs. This time, however, she had the return of her daughters as incentive to stay clean. Steve was reluctant to be fully responsible for Katrina; so I suggested that I become Katrina's legal guardian. Steve agreed and showed relief.

Steve was spending more and more nights at my house, but he occasionally needed to go to his house. Katrina missed him on the days he went home. She frequently wanted to go with him, but he was still concerned about his wife popping in unexpectedly and creating a scene. He was trying hard to be a good father.

Steve liked to cook, and he experimented with different recipes. Now when I came home from the office, there was the smell of food waiting for me and laughter or pleasant chatter between Steve and the kids. Since Steve was an engineer, he could have intelligent conversations with Ben, who was interested in higher mathematics.

Due to his increased drinking, he had missed several days of work, and despite his company's warnings, he'd walk into his office at any time he wanted, which could be 9:00 a.m. or noon. He was hardly an example or an inspiration to the young employees in his office. He was amusing since he always had interesting stories to tell of his past, and sometimes we would stay up until two or three in the morning talking and drinking beer. The difference between us was that I could get up early and still function. He could not.

One Monday morning Steve went into work and they told him to go home, that he no longer had a job. At first he couldn't believe it. After all, he was a good engineer. He had designed award-winning projects such as Water Country USA in Williamsburg, Virginia, as well as fish hatcheries and sewer treatment facilities. His work was highly praised.

When the reality set in, he expected to get another job without any difficulty. But the problem was that he never seriously looked. A friend of his found him a project as a private consultant, but he began not showing up for that project as well. He wasn't concerned. He had inherited some money after his father's death, and he took the attitude that when his money was gone, he'd look for another job.

Since he was spending a great deal of time at my place, he moved in. Although he was physically present, he did nothing. I'd come home tired and find dirty dishes were piled high in the sink; Katrina hadn't done her homework, and he didn't have the kids helping out. Katrina always found a reason to delay her bedtime. I believe he tolerated her manipulation out of guilt for not being previously involved in Katrina's life. This was not how I had raised Lil and Benjamin, and they began to resent Katrina and Steve.

Steve was often drunk when I came home, and he was sleeping later. His schedule was taking over, and I became resentful.

I'd tell Katrina that her responsibilities included doing chores and homework. She'd complain to Steve and would get out of her chores. She was dramatic, knowing that tears worked on her father's heartstrings, and she'd turn them off and on like a faucet. She'd generally ignore me and wait for her dad to awake and come to her rescue.

Shortly after Katrina began limited, supervised visitations with her mother, she wanted to return full-time to live with her. Katrina's sister Jane was at her mother's every other Saturday, and Katrina felt responsible for her and was afraid for her in her mother's environment. Steve and I didn't think Katrina should be put in the position of caretaker. Her mother still hadn't demonstrated stability—she wasn't looking for work or keeping her place clean of dog and cat feces.

Katrina ignored me one day, and I smacked her on her arm. She bolted out of the house and walked the few blocks to her mother's. Children's Services called Steve again. They wanted to interview him and me for child abuse. They asked me questions about my childhood and background, asking me about the quality of my relationship with my mother. After the interview Katrina came back to my house with us. Her plan to live with her mother hadn't worked.

Later in the year, Steve planned a trip to visit his brother in the Philippines. His brother was a great deal like him—both bull-shitters. While there he called us occasionally suggesting he may stay and work there and send for Katrina later. But nothing ever came of it, and after three months he returned and remained at my place.

In 1995 I insisted that he and Katrina live independently before the start of the next school year, but he ignored me. They stayed nine more months. Finally, I put all his things out on the sidewalk and told him if he didn't move, his belongings would be picked up by the trash collectors. He decided to move. We kept in touch by phone. Then I wrote him a letter telling him why I no longer wanted to maintain contact. I told him of some of the anger that had accumulated over the course of the relationship. In reality we were just drinking buddies.

Soon after that Katrina went back to live with her mother, Children's Services Agency was called again for neglect. This time they put Katrina and Jane into foster care, and later they were adopted by a family who lived far away from their mother. Steve, meanwhile, had obtained a job through a temporary agency working on an assembly line. Only by having to meet the responsibilities of living elsewhere did he begin to come back to life. One day on the job, he cut his hand, which ballooned up and turned black. They sent him to the hospital where he was diagnosed with cancer. When Katrina called and told me, I went to visit him, and he told me how my letter I wrote to him had killed him. I wasn't buying it; I was trying to heal myself. He never came home.

Katrina phoned a few months later and said they were giving him only days to live. I went to say goodbye, but he didn't recognize me. He must have weighed eighty pounds. Curled in a fetal position, he looked like a sonogram image. His obituary never appeared in the paper, and I suppose his wife purposely returned him to his hometown so neither Katrina nor I could attend any memorial service.

CHAPTER 38: THE TROUBLE WITH SECRETS

After Steve's death, I received a phone call from Samantha, a close college friend. We had kept in touch for over twenty years. Samantha was a nurse, and her husband, Russell was a prominent proctologist. She had been suffering domestic abuse for over five years. Samantha had decided to leave her husband, but had concerns over the turmoil he may cause for Kerri, their thirteen-year old daughter.

Kerri, was a vivacious youth and a good student. Recently she had withdrawn from friends and activities. Kerri was easily agitated. She exhibited erratic eating and sleeping patterns. Initially, Samantha attributed this decline to the parental conflict within the household. She asked me if I would allow Kerri to reside with me while she and Russell resolved their differences. I agreed out of friendship.

When she lived with me, I became aware that there were deeper problems. I noticed slash marks on her arms. This was even more alarming than other symptoms she had exhibited. I met Samantha for coffee and explained my concerns to her. While visibly shaken she appreciated my professional opinion. She listened as I told her about a local program for adolescents that could provide help for Kerri. Much to Samantha's relief, Kerri also realized she needed help and agreed to treatment. Under PA law a child over the age of fourteen has the right to refuse treatment. A day into the program, however, Kerri pleaded with her mother to take her home. Samantha was advised by the hospital staff to keep Kerri in the program. The following day she made progress by cooperating and learning to trust the staff. She attended therapeutic group activities and an individual session daily.

Two weeks later, while in a psychotherapy session Kerri divulged the secret long kept. She told her therapist, Rachel, that she had lied to her parents about spending a night at a girl friend's house. Instead, she and her friend went to a guy's house for a party. Unknown to the girls, there were older guys invited. The guys intoxicated Kerri and her friend with alcohol; both were raped.

"I had so much shame and guilt for what happened," Kerri sobbed. "I knew I was to blame for being where I shouldn't have been. The self-mutilation was a relief from the hurt of my inner pain." Rachel, procured Kerri's consent to have a family session. Rachel scheduled an appointment to include Kerri and her parents. It was apparent after a half-hour of mother and daughter waiting that Russell was not joining them. Rachel led into the session looking at Kerri and asking if she was ready to tell her mother "the secret". With tears streaming down her cheeks she told her mother of the traumatic event. Samantha rushed to Kerri and put her arms around her.

"Kerri, I feel horrible that you went through such an experience. Know that I am here for you. You did absolutely nothing wrong. Being at the wrong place at the wrong time never justifies anyone touching you in any way." They hugged and cried together. Rachel informed them of Kerri's legal right to press charges and made arrangements for Kerri to begin counseling with a rape-crisis professional once discharged from the program.

Kerri's discharge was delayed pending a meeting with her father to emphasize the seriousness of what Kerri was experiencing. When he had previously been informed of her self-mutilation, Russell had brushed it off.

"That's just something that teenage kids do for attention," he said. "It's no big deal." Russell attended the meeting with a condescending manner. He listened, but expressed no compassion or empathy. He was more concerned that Kerri had lied about her whereabouts on the night of the rape. Rachel explained that the symptoms that Kerri was manifesting were classic signs of a diagnosis of a sever clinical depression, secondary to acute post-traumatic stress disorder.

"The most effective treatment is therapy and a trial period of an anti-depression," explained Rachel.

"No child of mine needs medication," Russell responded gruffly, as he stalked out of the room.

Kerri was released and resided with me for a couple of months. Samantha resolved their marital difficulties, by filing for divorce and making arrangements for her and Kerri to live in peace.

CHAPTER 39: ME, MYSELF AND I

Benjamin met the love of his life while in high school, and after graduation they both enrolled at Syracuse University and moved to Syracuse, New York. Because I was unable to help him financially, he applied for grants and loans. He worked one semester, and took courses the next until he completed his degree.

Lilly experienced the challenges that adolescence entails. When she was fifteen she wanted to try a change and reside with Elliot. While I totally disagreed I had no legal grounds to stand on. This transition carried its' own problems as Lil attended a rural school district which, at that time, had no other Asian students. Lil felt isolated. She was frequently taunted by the other students. Frequently Elliot drove her to school, let her out at the front entrance, and she would walk to the back of the school and exit. She'd spend the day walking the rural roads, and return in time to be picked up at the end of the school day.

Lil returned to my house three months later. Two years later she graduated from her local high school. After a year in the work world, she decided she wanted to attend art school. She did so and excelled in her studies, landing a job before she graduated. While I was proud of her and happy for her future, I felt a void that I didn't express. My feeling, not expressed, manifested in sarcasm, curt remarks, and extreme sensitivity to anything Lil said or did.

"Mom," she asked. "Why are you always on my case? You should be happy for me. You act like you don't want me to leave. I'm not giving up my job in Atlanta to make you happy."

"I am happy for you," I cried. "Lil, I am going to miss you so much."

"I'll miss you too, but you've done such a good job with me, and I'm ready to move on." She reached for me with outstretched arms; we hugged as we brushed tears away. After she packed her final belongings in her car, we said our goodbyes. She handed me an envelope but requested that I open it later. As she drove away I opened the envelope; it was a poem that she wrote for me.

Visions

Across the ocean I flew

To land in your warm embrace.

In a garden of mysterious wonder,

We walk slowly amidst the gentle grace.

The storms come and go of course,
And lightning pierces the sky.
While the wind and rain tear through the trees
You hold me close as I tremble and cry.

When the sun breaks the clouds
and smiles from up above,
A realization comes to me from nowhere,
That storms are overcome by Love.

They say that hope is the golden key,
And strength is its brother.
Well, fate is what leads us through life,
And it was fate which made you my Mother.

I love you, Mom

XOXOXOXOXOXOXO

Love, Lilly.

I will never be more honored in my life.

My practice was growing. My business partner Dan and I bought a larger building, and we contributed equally to its expenses. Within the business, we each operated an independent practice. Dan and I shared the same easygoing temperament, and never had a conflict during the twenty years of our partnership. Dan, along with Dr. Jack Van Newkirk, the Superintendent of York City Schools, provided me with hope for the male population. I was fortunate to love my work, and it was easy to put in long hours.

I served on the York City School Board for twelve years, the last four as president. There were many committee meetings to attend as well as the actual board meeting. During the time I served, many changes occurred, such as the summer lunch program, all-day kindergarten, the option of year-round school, and the approval of charter schools. We were a dedicated group of nine members who, though not paid, formed policy and passed annual budgets of over $75 million. When we'd meet to discuss the annual budget there would only be a few members of the public attend; however, when we didn't appoint the same coach to the basketball team, we had to move the meeting to the high school cafeteria to accommodate the public attendance. When the board voted 5–4 not to rehire the coach, a minister in the community stood up and loudly damned us all to hell. Such was our reward for public service.

I traveled to many state and national conferences and workshops. I lobbied on Capitol Hill for educational reform and for more money in the education budgets. These years provided intellectual stimulation and a sense of helping others.

My tenure on the board included the years of my relationship with Steve as well as Lilly's critical teen years. I worked hard, but I enjoyed myself less. Sleep problems continued, my appetite was erratic, and during a two-year period I had gained fifty pounds. I was comforting myself with junk food and beer. My attention to household tasks waned. Although I had the money, I'd let bills accumulate without attending to such details as due dates. When I wasn't working, I didn't want to be bothered. Although many of the signs of depression were present, I did not recognize or heed them.

When I was in pain, I'd have a beer. When I was angry, I'd have a beer. If it was a time of celebration, I'd have a bottle of champagne.

I made an appointment with Dr. Jim, my family doctor. I told him my symptoms. He asked if I was seeking help and if I was still seeing Tom, my former therapist. He was unaware that Tom had died the previous September only a few days before I was to see him. Dr. Jim referred me to Selma, a psychologist who was also knowledgeable about mental health as well as drug and alcohol use.

I called that day and scheduled an appointment with her. At the first appointment, I explained that I was trying to understand what was going on in my life. I felt I should be feeling better since I was over a lot of conflict. I was sure that if I understood what was going on with me I could reason it away. Selma took some background information from me and did an initial interview. She told me to start keeping a journal and to begin writing an autobiography. She added that it didn't have to be a book. She also asked about my alcohol intake, and I was proud to tell her that I only drank beer, maybe two or three cans a day.

At the next appointment, I told her that I wanted to get on an antidepressant. She said she had no problem with that. I made an appointment with one of the psychiatrists in the same practice for the following week.

Before the day of my appointment with the psychiatrist, I attended a four-day continuing education course, Psychopharmacology, held in New York City. On Sunday morning I took the seven o'clock train from Lancaster to NYC, which allowed me to have some downtime before beginning the course on Monday. When I packed, I put a box of wine in a travel bag knowing how expensive wine would be in the City. This was a cost-saving measure.

The train stopped in Philadelphia for an hour before continuing to New York. I was enjoying the ride and enjoying getting out of town. Then I decided it would be nice to have a glass of wine while checking out the landscape. I carried my travel bag to the bathroom, and I poured a cup full of wine making sure the black lid was on the silver aluminum insulated cup. I returned to my seat and sipped the wine while gazing out the window.

When we stopped at the Penn Street station in New York, I took a cab to the hotel, checked in, and unpacked my bags. I propped myself up on the bed, turned on the TV, looked over the conference schedule, and had a glass of wine. I attended the conference in the morning, and when we broke for lunch, I had wine with my lunch. I was away from home and kicking back.

After the end of the first day, I bought a six-pack of beer before returning to my room. The next day was the same except I thought I would take in a play. I purchased a ticket for *Beauty and the Beast* and was fortunate in getting a seat fourth row center. I had my full cup of wine capped and safely out of sight under my raincoat. I wanted to be able to watch a Broadway play and have wine without anyone else being aware. By the time I left New York, I had finished the box of wine and then some. This had been a good break.

The next week I kept my psychiatry appointment. While the doctor strongly felt I was depressed, he requested one thing before he'd prescribe an antidepressant—that I not drink any alcohol for the next two weeks. *No problem—I can handle that.* He recommended that I dispose of any alcohol in the house. I had six cold beers in the refrigerator. *Surely, he did not mean I should waste these. When I drink these cold ones, I'll start my abstinence.* But the rest of the case was on the balcony. *Surely he didn't mean for me to pour the rest of the case down the drain. That'll be wasteful. I'll finish them over the next couple of days, and then I just won't buy any more*. I didn't buy any more beer.

I kept little hard liquor in the house, but I did have some Kahlúa from Mexico—*I might as well finish that*. So I did. I had no more alcohol in the house. *OK*, I thought, *I can do this*. Then the phone rang. It was Elliot's voice on the other end. I became angry, slammed the receiver in his ear, and automatically went to the fridge to get a beer. There wasn't any, and I was instructed not to drink until my appointment. I started pacing. *What to do with these angry feelings?* I noted in my journal.

My brother Ivan was an excellent beer drinker, sometimes having a case in a day. But he had quit, and I had taken him to an alcohol rehab where he completed a twenty-eight day program. He had stayed clean for about four years, had a relapse, and then went to another rehab, and remained sober. I knew he had a problem. I did not know I had one too.

When I had my next appointment with the psychiatrist, I told him I'd made it through the two weeks "without a problem," and he prescribed an antidepressant. He felt my use of alcohol at night was self-medication for my insomnia, and he prescribed a sleep aid. He diagnosed me with depression, anxiety, and attention deficit disorder, all secondary to posttraumatic stress disorder (PTSD) stemming from childhood trauma. He recommended individual therapy and told me that the PTSD would require therapy at different times of my life as flashbacks reoccurred.

At the next appointment with Selma, she mentioned that they had a group at her center that I probably could benefit from; I truly thought she meant professionally. She told me that it met three times a week for three hours; and between the group, I could meet with her individually for an hour. The next morning I went to observe. There were eight people sitting on chairs in a circle. As the group began, each person said his or her name followed by, "I'm an alcoholic." Then came my turn. I said, "My name's Julie, and I'm observing." I went to three groups and repeated this procedure.

When I saw Selma again, I told her I was through observing and that she was right—it was interesting.

"Did you see any similarities between the group and yourself?" she asked. Then it became obvious: she sent me to participate rather than to observe. *How could she say I was alcoholic?* I thought, *I was always at work and I only drank beer. I raised my kids, I took care of them, and I was very responsible. These drug and alcohol counselors really go overboard.*

"I have a brother," I told her, "who is an alcoholic, but not me."

"Are there other members of your family who drink excessively?" she asked.

"Two other brothers do, and one of my sisters do, but every one of us is responsible, have a good work ethic, and support ourselves. Therefore, none of us are alcoholics."

"That's interesting. And what were your adoptive parents' drinking habits?"

"My father would have a scotch and water in the two hours between afternoon and evening appointments, and usually two before dinner on a weekend. Occasionally my mom joined him for a drink on the weekends."

"Oh, so alcohol was present daily as your grew up?"

"I'm not sure where you're going with this, but my adoptive parents were not alcoholics."

"Nevertheless, they enjoyed their daily cocktails."

"Whatever," I said, as I rolled my eyes. "While your group has been interesting, I won't be returning."

"You've signed up for six weeks."

"What? How did that happen?"

"When you signed that stack of papers at the last session." *Shit, I signed each of the papers on the bottom line without reading them,* I thought.

"But I thought I was signing the confidentiality statement that I wouldn't divulge who I saw or what was said in the groups."

"Yes, that was one of the forms, but you also signed an agreement to treatment form."

"Really?" I winced.

"After this session you will no longer see me in individual session but will see Kevin, the counselor who runs the group." I was furious, but with my signature I'd made the commitment.

As I listened to the other group members day after day, I began to hear similarities between them and me. Many of them were raising families responsibly and going to work every day, but they were using alcohol as a way to cope with their feelings and as an escape measure. I learned that there are functional and dysfunctional alcoholics, but they are alcoholics nonetheless. Before long I heard myself say, "I'm Julie; I'm an alcoholic." I was beginning to believe it. Admitting it, though, did not stop me from resenting the disease. I was argumentative, and I sometimes mocked people in the group.

"I've attended nine AA meetings this week," announced one woman.

"Why?" I asked incredulously. "Don't you have a life?"The members of the group glared at me, and I remained quiet throughout the rest of the session.

I also felt that the drug and alcohol (D&A) program was identifying me as "bad." And I felt cheated that they didn't appreciate the adversity in my life I'd overcome. But in actuality a big part of my arrogant facade in the group was based on feeling shame. I didn't realize for some time that the program had nothing to do with blame or shame. One of the symptoms of being alcoholic is the denial of having a drinking problem. I certainly had that symptom. While I wasn't lying about drinking, I didn't admit it was causing problems in my life. Next to all the "real" problems in my life, drinking was at the bottom of the list.

While doing a family tree of alcoholism, it was clear that diagnosed or undiagnosed addiction was a multigenerational trait. Not all of my brothers or sisters were affected by addiction, but it was clearly present in the genes.

The program considered alcoholism as a disease and uses a twelve-step approach. The first step is admitting that we are powerless over the disease and that our lives have become unmanageable. I resented being accused of not having control over my life, and I truly felt I was managing just fine. I knew I was living independently, and I was the only one managing my life. *I never asked anyone for help. Who do they think they are, suggesting I have no control and am dependent?*

Everyone was assigned to complete a first step that involved listing five examples of times where using alcohol had potentially dangerous consequences. My list consisted of the following.

1. Driving under the influence
2. Driving under the influence with my kids in the car
3. Driving under the influence and taking another child to his or her home
4. Driving under the influence with a friend in the car
5. Driving under the influence with a flat tire to the next exit off of I-83 rather than pulling to the shoulder for help so a police officer wouldn't cite me for a DUI

As I read my list aloud, there was no way I could deny I had a problem. I also recognized that the only times I let my anger spew forth was after I'd had a few beers.

Another assignment was to bring a friend or family member to the session who had been affected by my drinking. That person would confront me about the times my drinking made him or her afraid, angry, or hurt physically or emotionally. B. J., a friend of mine, agreed to attend. She related that she was scared as I veered into oncoming traffic as I drank champagne while driving us to the airport bound for Cancun. She also described a night of drinking while in Cancun that ended with my sister and me skinny-dipping in the hotel pool and refusing to get out when security confronted us. We told them we were practicing for the Olympics and hadn't finished our practice yet. They escorted us to our room and we waited for them to get on the elevator before we returned to the pool. Her list went on and on. I knew I didn't want to put my friends and family in harmful situations—that wasn't me. I got a good look at the reality of my powerlessness.

During the family session, Lilly confronted me. She described times when I was drinking and would yell at her to do chores I wouldn't normally have asked her to do. She spoke of that same trip to Cancun and how embarrassed she was that I was her mom. I felt pain for what I had put others through, but this time I was handling the pain without being numb. Initially I was defensive.; *After all I have done for Lil, how could she throw those few times in my face?*

I still hadn't gotten it. This was not about blame or shame; it was about the reality of how my drinking had affected others. I tried to make myself feel better by pointing out that my family had not been deprived financially or materially and that I had not lost my home or job like some of the others in the group. But this was not about comparison. I had to make amends with my children. In so doing I learned humility, and I also realized how much I had to be grateful for. Not everyone had been as lucky as I was.

Recovery requires a change in the people, places, and things that are triggers for drinking: the familiar neighborhood bar, the drinking buddies, and the events that involve drinking all have to be changed. It was during this time that I was able to send Steve the final letter and keep him out of my life. The program sponsored some activities designed for fun that did not involve alcohol. One night I had a great time snow-tubing with the group. I hadn't done this before. There was a young woman at tubing who would occasionally bump into me or pull on my tube on the way down the hill. I didn't know anyone on the trip. I felt like a little kid all over again, except this time I was having fun.

The next morning the same young woman came to group. Her name was Dee. As soon as I saw her, I lit up; finally someone was coming in whom I could relate. And although I was almost fifty years old and she was only in her twenties, we became friends—my first new friend. We hung around in the group sessions and did things together on weekends. We kept each other company.

One weekend we went to Ocean City, Maryland, and decided to get tattoos. There had to be five hundred designs of all colors, shapes, and sizes on three of the walls. *Wow, I don't know what I want.* I thought. *I hadn't considered this. Maybe I should start by eliminating what I definitely don't want—I don't want the skull and crossbones or the cobra with the forked tongue, or the rat, or the heart with my lover's name, or the anchor....* Finally, I saw it. *That's the one!* I pointed to a design.

"I've made my choice—I want the cherub, but could you give her red hair and a couple of tears?" I asked.

Dee chose Winnie-the-Pooh carrying balloons, and she wanted him placed on her outer left leg just above her sock line. "Go ahead, you go first," she said to me."

Jake, the tattoo artist, put the picture of the cherub under some kind of imaging device and then made a stencil calculating the size in proportion to my shoulder. I followed him behind the partitioned curtain. I had to take off my blouse and remove my bra. I hadn't thought about that, but nineteen-year-old Jake graciously gave me a draped cloth to cover my chest as I leaned forward. The buzzing began as he etched the outline of the design; ninety minutes later he was still etching. Suddenly I was sweating and felt lightheaded. I endured it as long as I could, not wanting to wimp out.

"Jake, I think I'm about to pass out," I gasped.

"No problem, that's very common," he said. "I'll get you a cold compress.

"This is usual with the first tattoo," he said, handing me a towel. " On your next tattoo, your body will be used to the pain, and you won't have this reaction." *Next tattoo, right.*

Meanwhile, Jake's partner had arrived and was working on a body piercing behind the curtained partition next to me.

"Do I really have to put my feet in those stirrups?" the customer asked.

"Well I can't do your piercing where you've requested it if you don't."

"Aaaayeeeee." said the customer.

Oh shit, I'm at the point of no return.

Jake returned to his artistic endeavor and asked my color choices again. When he filled in the colors, he was proud of his work and asked if he could take a picture of it to add to his portfolio. *It must really look great—and to think my shoulder will be part of a portfolio. I'll probably see my cherub in ads or on TV, and I'll be able to tell myself that's* my *shoulder, and I created the distinctive red-haired cherub with the teardrops.* I agreed. Then he gave me a magnifying mirror so I could see the results.

"But it's so big!" I exclaimed. "It didn't look that big on the wall; it covers from mid-spine to my upper arm. I thought it would be a lot smaller."

"It looked smaller," Jake responded because it was among five hundred on the wall." I complimented him on his work, paid him the $185 plus a 10 percent tip, and walked out to the waiting room. I was surprised to see Dee there since I thought she was probably an art work in progress.

"Are you done already?" I asked.

"No," she said. "I decided that between your cold compresses and the screaming, I wouldn't get a tattoo." She had busted Winnie-the-Pooh's balloons.

Dee and I went to some AA meetings together, and there I met other people who were a lot like me. Everyone respected what the others had been through. No one made judgments or preached. People came to the meetings to gain what they needed for themselves. Fellowship was one of the pluses. In those weeks I learned about toxic shame versus healthy shame. I learned about setting boundaries between others and myself. I had no boundaries, which explained my susceptibility to being used by others who had no boundaries or being avoided by people who did have appropriate boundaries. I was getting along better with the group and went from that group into aftercare, which was a two-hour session once a week to reinforce the program.

My first day in aftercare, I sat next to a woman whom I knew from the first group. I wasn't sure what to do in the group; so I whispered and asked what was going on. I also didn't listen well when others were speaking. I showed it without knowing it by rolling my eyes or sighing that I was impatient. Toward the end of the first session, Ashley, the therapist, pounced on me.

"You're rude and arrogant," she yelled.

"Are you through yet?" I said. "I'm sorry I messed up your day."

"You don't have the power to mess up my day," she screamed.

I got up, stalked out of the room, and slammed the door. I cried on my drive home, intending to discontinue the "aftercare" program (I saw nothing caring about it). I felt I didn't deserve to be shamed after I worked so hard to gain self-confidence.

I was not aware of how my attitude affected others. I had felt secure in my dealings with people on a one-on-one basis, and I didn't have any experience or reference functioning as part of a group in therapy. I always avoided groups and prided myself on my independence. In my individual session with Kevin, he talked me into going back to aftercare. I returned and tried to figure it out. Ashley's initial reaction spurred me into action. As long as I was there, I resolved to do a good job. I completed all my assignments and volunteered at the beginning of the session to share my work. I got an AA sponsor and attended three to four meetings a week. I received respect within the six weeks of aftercare. With this phase completed, I was strictly on a one-hour individual session per week.

CHAPTER 40: GETTING REAL

I had a difficult time relating in therapy. I knew it would help me, it still felt like punishment. I had been in therapy before with Tom. During all I had been through in the previous two decades. but there was always some crisis that involved others. Now I was in therapy only for myself. I had difficulty making eye contact. I had difficulty responding to the simplest of questions. I was handling my feelings without alcohol, and I hadn't the foggiest notion what to do. If it wasn't a question I could handle by thinking, I went blank. Sometimes I could sense the invisible wall from my early childhood that kept me from feeling; it kept me silent. As I drove back home from the session I began thinking: *I'm really stupid for not being able to come up with anything.* I wasn't trying to be resistant. Without realizing it I was using a defense mechanism called disassociation, since the feelings were so overwhelming. Zoning out, or going numb, kept me feeling safe, and it happened automatically.

For my assignments in-between appointments, I continued to write daily in my journal since more feelings automatically emerged as I wrote rather than thought. My journal became a part of my session; as I read it aloud, Kevin helped me process the feelings connected with some horrendous events in my life. He encouraged me to write letters to some of the people who were adults at the time so I could vent my feelings and realize I was not responsible for their actions.

"These people are dead; they won't get the letter," I said.

"The letter is not about them receiving and responding to it," Kevin told me. "It's for you to return the responsibility to whoever owns it. Forgiving is not to give approval for wrongdoing, but rather it is for giving back to the owner." Having reviewed my journal, Kevin told me to write a letter to my father and let him know how it felt to view autopsies as a kid. I was diligent about assignments and recorded the following in my journal to discuss at my next session:

Upon Seeing Autopsies as a Child

Dad:

Last night I read the following in *Trauma and Recovery* by Judith Herman: "The traumas which are most significant are those which consist of the witnessing some specific event: a mutilating death, or accident, operation, abortion or birth in the home."

You took me to see autopsies. I am enraged. You as a medical doctor knew damn well the horror of that for kids. That was the only one-on-one time we had! That was our "quality time"! I would hear the phone ring, hear your part of the conversation, and "just happened" to be at the back door so I could ask to go with you—and you let me!

I was really scared of those dead naked people, but because I wanted to mean more to you than my sisters, I pretended to be interested. You let me pretend!

You slit the body right down the middle with your sharp scalpel. To this day I can smell the embalming fluid. I didn't know how wrong all this was, but you did—Mom had to know too. Why was nobody protecting me from horror?

I'm angry as I see the scenes of you showing me the organs of the body, letting me touch them and hold them if I wanted. I couldn't get myself to do that. *Just watch and turn off any fear, any disgust, or any embarrassment*. Then I'd watch you stitch the skin with a big needle and thread—like Mom hemming my dress. All I had to do was to pretend it wasn't real, and it got easier to do that by going somewhere else even though I stayed in the same room.

For some of the autopsies, you drove thirty miles each way. I wanted you to talk about regular stuff, like I heard some children's dads do. If there was any talk, it was about the dead body and you finding the cause of death. However, I'd go home happy and brag to my sisters about our time together.

When I look at that now, I think that act is something that would come under torture. I can now understand why I would never watch scary movies. What could be scarier than what I had seen? I was scared of everything, but I couldn't admit that to you. You wouldn't like me if I was scared of things.

I get the image of a truly sick person when I think of the things you did. But of course you were the coroner's physician, prison physician, surgeon, owner of his own hospital, art collector, philanthropist and, as we were told over and over, the rescuer of girls from the orphanage and loved by everyone. Why did you adopt no boys, only girls? Most fathers want at least one son.

It's strange. I find myself looking at this scene, and I'm having a hard time expressing my contempt. You robbed me of my childhood. I've looked at what I've written and it feels surreal—that I must not have lived it because I can't imagine that someone would knowingly do this to even the most evil of people. Cruel doesn't describe it—they were *real people* you were cutting up—and I was a *real kid*, only five, six, seven, eight—not a medical student. I don't know when you stopped taking me with you, but I know at the time I felt a loss, as if I wasn't good enough for you to spend time with.

I'm feeling weak and nauseous as an adult writing about this. I can't believe, and yet I know it to be true, that you exposed me to this atrocity. It did happen—you did it and Mom said nothing. I'm having a hard time now, and I'm just feeling numb. The invisible shield is back.

Your adopted daughter,

Julie

And for myself I wrote:

Stitches of Feelings

There are feelings that I thought I put away forever
But now they come hurling back at me
At speeds of at least two hundred mph.

It is as though
They are mad at me for leaving them alone for so long.

They tell me I should have listened to them then.
I should have watched over them or
At least looked in and checked them occasionally.
But I never did.
The way I remember is they hurt.

Take the feeling of fear, for instance.
That really hurt.
What hurt most about fear was
People who told you that your fears weren't real.

They said:
"You're being silly."
"Big girls aren't afraid."
"Grow up,"
"It's your imagination."

It wasn't my imagination
Or maybe it was.

But anyway
My fears were real.

I wanted to grow up.
I didn't want to be silly.
And I wanted my father to love me.
He could only love strong people.

So I became afraid of nothing.
I practiced walking in the dark
By closing my eyes in the daylight.
And I wasn't afraid of the dark.

I started believing in reincarnation—
And I wasn't afraid of dying.
I made the "Boogie Man" into a clown
And I wasn't afraid to walk by that closet
Where they told me he lived.

I grew wings like the Angels

And I wasn't afraid of falling.

I put on a suit of armor

And I wasn't afraid of anyone hurting me.

So I gave up my fears.

At least Dad must have thought I gave them up.

He said later,

"You are the brave one in the family."

But sometimes

The reality of my fears as a child

Come charging back at me.

And I remember

The terror,

The screams,

The tears,

The pleas,

The helplessness.

But most of all

I remember

The loneliness of being afraid.

Kevin was astonished with my writings; now *he* was the silent one.

CHAPTER 41: PERCHANCE TO DREAM

Not many months into treatment, I began having intense dreams. I had a dream of going out onto the porch of a rustic home in the woods. There was a beautiful clay pot of purple tulips; but as I looked at them, the flowers turned to dead rats connected to each other in the pot. I was frightened. That was the first time I associated feelings in a dream. I found it was a lot easier to talk about my dreams since I wasn't threatened by the feelings. I began to keep a journal of my dreams.

In my twenties I often dreamed in animation, and Bugs Bunny was a frequent nighttime visitor. Shortly after I reunited with my siblings and had heard stories of my father, Yosemite Sam—complete with guns, holster, and red bushy mustache—appeared in my dreams. Snow White (a symbol for my mother) was hosting a formal cocktail party, and Yosemite planted himself in the middle of the double staircase, lit tissues on fire, and dropped them on unsuspecting guests. Bugs Bunny (me) raced up the stairs telling him to stop, but the potential guns frightened me, and I froze mid-staircase.

In my thirties and forties, I didn't pay attention to my dreams since daytime was more than enough to handle. Now in recovery, I took a serious look at my dreams, which contained stored emotions in abundance. Dreams—wonderful, frightening, colorful dreams. Dreams were my subconscious working while I wasn't on guard. They were a mixture of day residue and unresolved issues—I had plenty of material. After one powerful dream in December 1990, I wrote the following:

Letter to Adopted Parents

> I had a dream the other night that's been on my mind ever since. My emotions are feeling faster than I can process. In the dream I'm lying back in a small boat and having fun in calm waters. We're heading to a tropical beach, which is in front of us. The island is to my right, and the sun is shining over it.
>
> We hear a storm warning, and to the left of me is black water, and the twenty-foot waves are pitching

violently. The sky is extremely dark. I see an ocean liner with a single couple standing on the top deck in formal wear. It is the two of you—my adopted mother and father staring into the distance like statues.

The loudspeaker announces that the powerful storm is endangering the ship and asks if we want to help the crew—if so, speak up now.

As I see you as a couple, I feel a powerful magnetic draw to be with you, although I would clearly be in danger. *If something is going to happen to them*, I thought, *it should happen to me also.*

I yell, "I want to go." I am propelled along with rescue workers through a tunnel under the sea to the luxury liner.

Now out of the dream it occurs to me how duty-bound I felt in the dream—as if I owe you my life and happiness. It's making me angry to think how much you took from me. I didn't and don't owe you anything. Some of the anger is that you never told me otherwise. You reinforced the idea that indeed you had rescued us from the orphanage and from our parents, who in your words were just "white trash." I was ten years old, Mom, when you said that. It was the first time I heard "trash" used with people. An image I had was the rusty metal incinerator can far away in the backyard that was used to burn trash, and I thought maybe I should be there.

I gave up any identity of me. I was totally lost in the two of you. *Am I making them proud? Will they still like me? How can I get them to be glad they adopted me? I owe them* so *much.*

Dad, you said, "Take a goddamn bastard out of the orphanage, and this is how I get repaid."

I thought, focused, and concentrated daily. *If I just do good things for other people, I will make up for me.* I was always reaching out, always doing good deeds for everyone else. I don't remember doing anything for me.

Mom, you said, "If it hadn't been for us, you'd still be sitting your ass at the orphanage—nobody else would have wanted you." The message was clear—I owe. I owe you my life; I owe you my existence. I owe, I owe, so off to please I go.

Oh, and that wonderful comment directed to me: "You can't make a silk purse out of a sow's ear." How cruel! What gave either of you the right to give me that shit?

I took the helping role with Jeannie because that obviously pleased you. You owe *me* for all those years I was her caretaker and nobody's kid. You let me be "nobody's kid" throughout my "kid hood." How old was I when that began—four years old? And you just let me do it. I woke up to take Jeannie to the bathroom so she wouldn't wet the bed. I got a few good comments for that. Maybe that was the start of my sleep problems. I never set an alarm to wake up to take her to the bathroom; I just conditioned myself to automatically wake up once in the night. What is normal about that?

I thought I was grieving about people leaving me—about abandonment and rejection issues—but maybe some of the grieving is for the self that I abandoned for the sake of you two. Each of you extracted much from me. I had no self. I had only your selves. I resent that you encouraged and allowed me to forsake myself.

The twenty-foot waves in the dream represent the constant unrest that I felt. My resentment was that you had to know it was wrong. You had to know the *me* you created wasn't natural. I never remember being a kid's kid, but I do remember so often being an adult as a kid. I would act, react, and think things through so often as if every little detail mattered. When I set the table, I made sure the edges of the napkins met exactly, pressing down the creases over and over. Should I fold it vertically? Does horizontal look better? Should I make it a triangle? And I tried these options over and over again, never being sure it was perfect. Then I had to be sure that the forks were the same distance from the left of the plate as the spoons were to the right, measuring the distance using the prongs of the fork. Then I had to make sure that I had set both of your places exactly the same so neither of you would think I liked the other one better. With my sister's places, I would not be so exact and think I was getting away with something.

When I heard the question from the next room, "Julia, why is it taking so damn long for you to set the table?" I would try to hurry but start to cry in frustration that it wouldn't be right. Then at dinner I would wait for comments, but I learned that if I heard nothing, then I had done it right.

Now I am angry that neither of you said, "Julia, it's no big deal. You don't have to be perfect for us to keep you—your worth lies in you and we love you."

Your adopted daughter,

Julie

CHAPTER 42: GIFTS

A floodgate had been unleashed. I continued writing letters, writing journals, and attending AA meetings. At the suggestion of my sponsor, Patricia, I attended the Women's Recovery Retreat, which was at Camp Hebron in Peter's Mountain in Pennsylvania in 1997. I didn't know what to expect, but I was open to suggestions.

The weekend was scheduled in late fall. The topic was Prayer and Meditation. *Great,* I thought, *I'll take my Walkman along, and I'll be able to listen to the Penn State game while overlooking the fall foliage.* But that image was shattered when I received the list of rules with my receipt of payment, which prohibited the use of electronic devices over the weekend. *Wait a minute—recovery is one thing, but I can't miss a game this late in the season.*

In the past I hadn't gone to any women-only meetings. I felt that a mixed group was more interesting, and that I might meet a man who was also in recovery. I phoned Rhonda, a new friend, who was going to the retreat and asked if she wanted to ride with me. Rhonda was much younger than I was and she liked to laugh. She accepted the invitation. But when I picked her up, she wasn't feeling well and slept while I drove. When we arrived at the camp, she dashed from the car to the retreat house, claimed a room for us, and promptly went to bed where she remained most of the weekend. *Great,* I thought, *here I am with fifteen women for the weekend, none of whom I know. And for this I'll miss the game?*

I answered a knock on my door and met Daisy, a tall woman who knew Rhonda and wanted to say hello. I told her Rhonda was ill and asleep, and I introduced myself. She invited me to come across the hall and meet Marti, her roommate. The three of us hit it off. All three of us liked to play; and by the evening's end, Daisy and I had short-sheeted Marti's bed. After we giggled over that, we went outside in our pajamas, made rustling noises, and occasionally threw pebbles at windows. As a result of our mischief, a curfew was announced at the next morning's meeting.

During the lunch break, Marti and I went to the camp gift shop and loaded up on toys. Rubber snakes, spiders, Styrofoam airplanes, yo-yos, and a jar of bubbles were among our treasures.

That night it was Daisy who shrieked when she discovered a "snake" lying somewhere beneath her covers and fortunately her scream was before curfew. *This must be what it would have felt like to have gone to summer camp*, I thought. Although I didn't get to hear the Penn State game, I enjoyed the fellowship of the retreat. I found spirituality and had fun—with women no less! Marti and Daisy lived close to me in York, and we kept in touch in-between fall retreats.

The following year at the retreat, we had a minister as the facilitator. Her name was Pastor Joan. I felt drawn to her energy. I participated in the spiritual readings and workshops, and I felt like I had known Joan all my life. She was a blue-eyed blond, and she displayed compassion as she listened to the women describe the events that brought them into recovery. That night I had a weird sensation; I wanted to go downstairs to her room and just sleep on the floor next to her bed. She reminded me of my mother. As she led other workshops that weekend, I arrived early so I could have the seat next to hers in the circle. In her last workshop of the weekend, she told us to write a letter to ourselves from God. We had to think about what God would say to each of us about our lives, and we were to write it spontaneously.

Dear Julie,

> I know you have every reason to believe that I had deserted you when you were very young and in the care of people who represented me on earth—the nuns. How could you ever believe that anyone but yourself was there for you? You were ridiculed by them, you were sexually and physically abused by them, and they separated you from the other children. They shamed you when they put those red socks on you that told the other children you were from the devil and they weren't to play with you. It must have seemed to you that I wasn't there for your brothers or sisters either as they were put in front of other children at the orphanage and called heathens because the authority was Catholic and all of you were Protestants.
>
> I know I let you down many more times in elementary school when nuns who cast themselves as

my representatives mistreated you. I want you to know how false they were—they had absolutely nothing to do with me. But how could you have known that at age four when all you had in all the world to believe in was them? They were horrible, cruel people. They were truly unhappy people.

You are a survivor, and now you can see them for what they were—and hopefully you are forgiving enough that now that the truth is known—you can forgive me and realize that I have always been here for you, but you were so busy trying to be "right" for all those humans that you didn't look behind you.

Let go of those people and know that I will protect you.

Respectfully,

God

I felt like a burden had been lifted. We ended the retreat by forming a circle of arms across shoulders and singing "Lean on Me." The following day I looked up Pastor Joan's phone number. She lived in my same county. So I called and asked if we could meet for coffee. She agreed. When I arrived at the coffee house, Joan waved me over to her table, and as we talked a friend of hers named Aisha entered and gave a hearty "Hi, Joan." She joined us. I liked the wonderful lilt in her voice and her wide smile. Her sense of humor was evident, and that was the beginning of a long-term friendship with both Joan and Aisha.

In 1997, I made the decision not to run for a spot on the school board. Twelve years was enough civic duty for any person. I also decided to sell my house and downsize from the big house, which required a lot of maintenance, to a smaller townhome. I enjoyed the familiarity of my neighborhood and wanted to remain in it. I walked through my neighborhood, with a realtor and a block and a half later, I found my new house. I signed the agreement to buy before I put my house up for sale.

Everything worked out, and I found a buyer. On the settlement date, I was to receive the money from my house at 10:00 a.m. and buy the new one at 11:00 a.m. But that day my realtor informed me there was a glitch. When the legal distribution of property between Elliot and me took place ten years before, Elliot's lawyer had trusted him to file the necessary papers in the courthouse to transfer the jointly held deed to my name alone. Elliot had never done that, and as a result I was selling property that still belonged to him. Frank, my realtor, drove to Elliot's office to have him sign it. Elliot knew he would be in legal trouble if he didn't sign; nevertheless, Elliot let Frank sit in his waiting room for hours before signing the papers, and thus delayed the transfer of both properties. It was twelve years after the divorce, and he still had to exert one final show of power and control. Both properties transferred the following day.

CHAPTER 43: ENCOURAGEMENT

Newton Avenue was perfect, tucked securely within half a block of four major streets with enough distance to provide privacy from street traffic, glaring lights, and noises. It created a safe haven for me.

I bought *The Courage to Heal Workbook* by Laura Davis, which is for survivors of child sexual abuse. I began the activities in the book in earnest. A preliminary recommendation was to build a circle of support from people who knew you were working on this issue; people with whom you could safely talk with as you did your work. When I identified my circle, I asked them to write a few words of support for me in the front pages of my workbook and sign their names. In the center of the page, I wrote my own note to me: "I would hate to be at another point in my life looking back, knowing that I could have made it better for me, but didn't. Change is made possible through problems—adversity propels."

I'd open my book and gain internal strength knowing I had wonderful family and friends supporting me in my recovery. Of all the notes, the most meaningful one came from my son, Benjamin:

Mom,

I am proud of you for all you have achieved in helping others and yourself. I am a prime example of your generosity and love, which you do not take enough credit for. When you get stuck, think of those great deeds to move on. It's not easy to mend one's soul, so take it one emotion at a time. If you need any support, I'm one of the many who are willing to be at your side.

With much love,

Benjamin

Then he added, "'No one can belittle you without your permission'—Eleanor Roosevelt."

I picked a specific person who was also a survivor and asked her to write me a letter of encouragement that I could paste in my workbook. Although I had only known Joan for a few months, I asked her. I received the letter of my lifetime and hope everyone has such a note of inspiration.

Dear Julie,

A letter of encouragement—what can I say to someone who has survived more in her lifetime than most of us can understand? All I can say is that when I think over the people I know and admire, I would put you at the very top of the list. Not only have you survived but you have persevered. You have conquered incredible odds and horrendous abuse, and in doing so you have risen above it to bring love to others and make history in our community.

You know, some of us are born to be survivors. For some mystical and seemingly magical reason, we are able to rise above the circumstances of life and respond positively to the world around us. Not only have you responded positively to your world but you have in many ways made that world a better place.

Federico Fellini once said, “There is no end. There is no beginning. There is only the infinite passion of life.” How true that rings for those of us who have lived and persevered “through many dangers, toils, and snares.”

And through the amazing grace of God we can say we have already come this far and we are moving on—we have been blessed with the crucibles that have been able to absorb the unjust pain of life and transfer it into life-giving fire that has touched the lives of others with good and love. The infinite passion of life is something for us to relish because the never-ending circle begins with being and continues with being. For you, it’s being Julie Swope!

This letter is written to encourage you to strive to relish every moment of life and to encourage you to continue to unleash the healing power that lies within you—to encourage you to heal and in healing grow closer to God and closer to yourself—to fully discover who you are and to enjoy getting to know the Julie of all ages.

For some reason, God chose you and me, and all other survivors for special tasks—some of us choose to listen and some don't. It's probably good that we don't know what the next day will bring; we might question our capabilities, but God never does. In fact God has more faith in us than we have in God. And there is a message written on our hearts and in our lives that the world—our own special world—is to read. It is a message of love.

Gandhi said that his life was a message. Our lives are our messages. Your life is your message, and it is a message of victory. He also said, "Let our first act every morning be this resolve: I shall not fear anyone of earth. I shall fear only God. I shall not bear ill will toward anyone. I shall conquer untruth by truth and in resisting untruth, I shall put up with all suffering." When we know the truth, we are set free—to be whatever we want to be. It's our choice!

The truth is that you are lovable and you are wonderfully made; as you heal, tell yourself that you love you—each and every morning. Look in the mirror and say, "I love you, Julie Swope! You have been created perfect in the image of God."

This is the last year of the first half of the first century of your life—it is a time of celebration and historic achievement—and all of that was done while you were one of the walking wounded. Can you even imagine what you will accomplish when you have healed completely? The truth is you are healed—you were healed the day you decided to heal—and the days to come are simply steps in claiming that healing. It may seem like Friday, but Sunday's a coming, and Sunday is resurrection—your resurrection to freedom, joy, and love! You can do it. And remember—I'm here to help!

Finally, I want to share a quote from Kathleen Norris's book, *Dakota: A Spiritual Geography*: "In our century, Carl Jung has reminded us that to grow we must eventually stop running from our 'shadow' and turn to face it. Around the time I joined my grandmother's church, I dreamed of a fundamentalist minister and his flock had surrounded my house threatening to bury me alive under a truckload of rocks and dirt. I sat inside, feeling helpless as they sang hymns and shouted curses. Finally, however, I went outside to face them. I ordered them to leave, and woke up feeling as if a great weight had been lifted from me" (99).

The day will come when you give the order! Until then the struggle continues—blessed be God.

Peace, joy, love,

Joan

Joan also moved to Newton Square within a year, and Aisha moved to an apartment only a block away from us. Sometimes Aisha and I went for bike rides on York's rail trail, and I'd smile broadly as Aisha passed me with her Muslim veils flying in the wind. When I'd catch up to her, we'd sing John Denver songs as we rode—"Country Roads" and "Annie's Song" were our favorites. Sadly, Aisha died in 2004. An hour after hearing of her death, I was sitting at my computer, and out of the corner of my eye, I saw something flutter by. Even though it was winter, a pale-yellow butterfly with two small black dots on each wing was on my floor. I placed a piece of paper under her gossamer wings, slid her into a jar labeled "Hope," and preserved Aisha. When I open the jar, energy floats into the air and I smile.

CHAPTER 44: STRINGS ATTACHED

On New Year's Eve 1999, I attended First Night York, a local celebration, with my best friends, Joan, Patricia, and Aisha. I had some free time in my life and knew I wanted to take up a new musical instrument, but I didn't know which one. This was the perfect venue to sample musical instruments. I observed each entertainment group and visualized the instrument and myself, taking note of the size and tone of the instrument and whether it "felt like me." *The flute has an airy sound and could be me; the clarinet and oboe have a mellow, earthy sound, but I am not "windy." The trumpet, French horn, and saxophone—too brassy, unlike me. The violin was a definite maybe; the dulcimer perhaps, but I don't get hammered anymore.*

By eleven o'clock Patricia bid us all a happy New Year and went home to bed. Aisha and Joan left to attend services at the mosque, and I remained downtown to see the fireworks usher in the millennium. There was one more musical performance to see. It was a harpist. I listened, and within the first minute, the harp called to me. So many times we say, "I want to do this, I want to do that," but time passes, and we never do what pleases us. The harp called me, and I answered.

I never realized that harps came in different sizes since I only knew of the concert pedal harp. Though always mesmerized by the sound, I knew that, because of my size, I could never play it. The performer wasn't much bigger than I, and she had three different sizes of lever harps on stage. She invited the audience to try them. I took her up on the offer and gingerly approached the stage. While everyone else asked questions, I walked around the harps to check them out from each angle.

"Would you like to try them out?" Shawn, the performer asked me.

"They're so beautiful and delicate," I said. "I'm afraid I might break the strings."

"They're not that delicate; the strings are made for plucking." She plucked "Country Gardens" and then glided her fingers up and down the strings to make the sounds of "harps in heaven."

"Go ahead—try it," she said.

Although my plucks sounded like plinks, I was sold. She introduced me to her husband, David, who made the harps that were on stage. I took her card, phoned her on Monday, and had my first lesson the following Wednesday. Shawn gave lessons in her "harp mobile," a van transformed into a musical studio, and we met in the parking lot of City Island in Harrisburg, Pennsylvania. We discussed her fee and the costs of lessons, music books, a stand, a bench, and the harp rental. By the end of the lesson, I told her I wanted to order a harp. She advised me to wait, but I told her that I was positive and I didn't want to miss out on my "calling."

I used her rental harp called Black Licorice, and five months later my harp of cherrywood was born; when it arrived I named it Cherry Jubilee. I felt like a kid again taking my first piano lesson. I committed myself to weekly lessons and practiced every day. I completed all of my assignments in my note spellers and workbooks, as well as the music. I began with "Twinkle, Twinkle, Little Star." I wasn't a natural, and didn't want to play for anyone. But when a couple of my friends insisted I play for them, I'd ask them to go the next room to listen because I didn't want to be watched while I played. That old fear of making mistakes had crept back into my life even though my instructor and my support group encouraged me, praised me, and said what a wonderful sound I made.

The harp soothed my "savage soul" and was my therapy at the end of the day after listening to clients. Joan had formed a women's group. At one of the monthly meetings, each person was to bring something to share; I took the plunge and brought my harp. I played three songs with my right hand only. First I played "White Choral Bells" and "Long, Long Ago," and then I told the group that my final number was for any recovering alcoholics in the group—"Drink to Me Only with Thine Eyes." With a racing heartbeat, red blotches, and sweating, I persevered.

A few months later, I discovered I could use the harp to express my feelings. I began composing music and writing lyrics for my "inner child." I wrote a tender lullaby for her, "Dreamscape," which led me back to writing as therapy. I wrote the following fantasy letter and signed it *Dad*:

To Julie, from Dad

Dear Julie,

I regret departing this earth with so many things left unsettled. I am in hell now, so I have a lot of time to think about past transgressions. I have at least ten thousand letters to write to express my acknowledgment of my responsibility for some of the hell on earth you have gone through.

I was wrong to use your innocent trust, your innocent need of acceptance, affection, and connectedness. I was wrong to use your fears of rejection and abandonment. I was wrong to place my selfish physical needs above yours to the extent that I totally negated any right you had to even have needs, let alone have them met. I was wrong to cut off your feelings and have you consider only mine.

I could see clearly that you were starving emotionally, yet I used that to feed my own hunger. In so doing, I made you feel you were invisible while

I gained more power in your eyes. I towered over you, crushed you, and then expected you to give me more; you did because that is how much you wanted to feel truly loved by me.

I was wrong to give you such a blatantly distorted view of love. I was wrong for not showing you what a good father is. I was wrong for not picking you up and letting you sit on my shoulders to watch a parade, for not carrying you to bed and reading a story to you, and for not saying prayers with you. I was wrong for not showing you how to build sandcastles or taking you to meet the ocean. I was wrong for never helping you with your homework, for never playing ball, and for never flying a kite with you, finding gold at the end of the rainbow.

I was wrong for yelling, cursing, and being so physically threatening that you were scared to approach me. I was wrong for being absent so much, for never participating, for not being there for First Communion or Confirmation and for always sending substitutes in my place—even sending the butler to take you to the circus.

I was wrong for taking you to see autopsies. I was so in love with my own skills and importance that I never even considered the effects this would have on you. All I knew was how starved you were to spend time with me and I didn't consider what a bizarre way for a child to spend time with her father. I was the sick one. You were healthy—with your need of wanting to feel connected. I must give you credit for perseverance; while I would have totally ignored you, you sought me fervently. I was wrong to confuse you about affection, acceptance, and self-worth being linked so closely with pleasing me sexually. That clearly was a damaging thing to do to an innocent victim. You were too young to separate it all out, and I was of a nature where I wouldn't have wanted you to figure it out—such was the depth of *my* pathology.

Through this letter I want to define my wrongs and I own them as strictly mine—*not yours.* There was never anything wrong with you—you were an innocent, trusting child. As for me, I am in a place where I deserve to be.

If reincarnation exists, I will know how to be a good father in my next life.

Be healthy,

Dad

I entered a new relationship—with the harp—but this time I knew there were strings attached.

CHAPTER 45: SOUNDS OF SILENCE

Although the harp was excellent therapy for me, it didn't increase my confidence to play in public; nor did it help me feel at ease during lessons. Shawn was taking a sabbatical and referred me to another teacher. Although he was as laid back as Shawn, I continued having anxiety during lessons. In addition I had experienced some frightening flashbacks and wanted help in processing them.

I called the psychology office where I met my first therapist, Tom. I credited him with being the savior of my sanity during the course of my marriage and divorce. I had missed him so much over the years after his death. I had a difficult time returning to Tom's office. In my first session with Glenn, who was part of the practice with Tom, I shed a few tears. Glenn said he missed Tom too.

"What brings you in?" he asked.

"I take weekly harp lessons," I said. "I've have two different teachers who are nice and not intimidating in the least, but I get anxious when they watch me play, and I make mistakes during lessons that I don't make while practicing."

"I can help you," Glenn said, "with cognitive techniques such as thought stoppage, deep breathing, and self-talk."

"But I'm a shallow breather, and I can't relax enough to take a deep breath. But with your help I'll give it a try."

"Good. Now briefly tell me about your childhood." I lost eye contact with Glenn and stared into nothingness during a few minutes of silence.

"It's the word 'briefly' I'm having trouble with," I said.

"Or, not so brief," Glenn said.

"It was complicated, and I know we're running out of time. And I've had four frightening flashbacks involving mutilation and dead animals. Can we start there next week?" He agreed, and we scheduled the next visit for the same time the following week.

At the next session, I told Glenn of the day during the previous summer when a tree had uprooted in my yard. I dug a deeper hole to put the Japanese cherry tree back in place and anchor it. As I dug, I noticed some roots in the ground the same color as the streaks on the shell of my box turtle. I concluded in a flash that I had split my turtle in half. I felt anguish, panic, and guilt; I had just murdered my pet.

I was ashamed to tell anyone at first. Finally when I quit sobbing, I told a few close friends, but no one understood my distress. I had killed my pet! I felt my skin oozing with shame. I took a shower, but as much as I scrubbed, I still felt dirty. That afternoon, Lilly visited me. I sobbed as I told her what I had done.

"It's OK, Mom," she said. "You didn't mean it; it was only an accident. You would never harm your turtle." Then her friend entered my kitchen holding something in the air.

"Is this the turtle you killed?" he asked with a grin.

He held my turtle, which was kicking in the air. My turtle was whole and alive! *How did she come back to life?* I thought. I returned to the hole I had dug and took a closer look, and I saw a mixture of dead leaves and split tulip bulbs. Only then did I realize I had experienced a flashback.

Another flashback I relayed to Glenn involved the time in the fall when I opened my shed in the back yard and thought I saw a dead mouse. I screamed and slammed the door. I called my son Andrew to come and remove it. He entered the kitchen.

"Mom, here's your mouse," he said, as I shrieked and jumped back. "No, Mom, look at it; it's a flat, gray stone that was on the floor in the shed."

"You must not have seen the one I saw," I said. "Go back and look again; I want it out of there."

"I had the light on when I saw this; there is nothing else there," he replied.

"Well, look at the shape and color of the stone. Can you at least see why I thought it was a mouse?" I said sheepishly. Glenn listened patiently as I recounted this experience, observing my terror in relaying the events.

At another session with Glenn, I relayed another flashback experience. In the house where I used to live, the cat came through the pet door with a partially dead bird. I ran into my bathroom and slammed the door. When I heard the cat and bird bumping around in the bedroom, I was too scared to come out. I opened the bedroom door a crack and screamed, mistaking the dead bird for a rat. I summoned my courage. With that, I took a running leap to my balcony door and never looked in my bedroom. Once outside and down my back steps, I felt safe. I called Andy from my office to drive to my house, take the rat out of my bedroom, and dispose of it. He did so and commented later that he had found a dead bird in my bedroom. I realized then that I'd had another flashback; however, to be safe, I boarded up the pet door.

Over the months with Glenn, I was able to talk about something I had never told anyone. Since I was a child, I'd had repeated flashbacks of being buried underground: I feel fur and feathers around my face and in my mouth. I smell blood. Then someone reaches for me; I don't see a face—just a large hand. Whenever the flashback occurred, I tried to suppress it. I felt slimy talking about it, but it returned again and again. The actual experience occurred before I was adopted, but I don't know if it occurred at the orphanage or earlier. I do know that I had developed a fear of dead animals before I was adopted. I vividly remember the night my grandmother watched us, and the cat brought a mouse to my bedroom. The terror jumps back at me as if it were happening now.

When I was forty-five years old, I saw a bone specialist because my wrists hurt when I carried anything heavy, such as a six-pound bowling ball. He told me that both of my wrists had been seriously dislocated at a young age when my bones were still forming. The right one was more distorted than the left. Since it interfered with my ability to function, he suggested surgery and removed the bone.

"Your flashbacks are all of terror," said Glenn. "Do you see any symbolism between them and your life?

"I think the dead turtle was about looking at the dead bodies my father autopsied," I said. "When I was six or seven I would look down at the dead bodies and I thought somehow I killed them."

"And you've carried that guilt all these years," Glenn softly replied. "And now you can give back the guilt, knowing it was never yours to begin with." I breathed a deep sigh of relief.

Although I'll never know exactly what happened to me at a very young age, I was relieved to recount these events and flashbacks, and have a witness to my pain. Glenn stated that our bodies remember everything that ever happened to us, even when our minds protect us by shutting out painful events. Glenn didn't have me committed, and I wrote the following poem for the next session.

Screams of Silence

My eyes saw what my voice couldn't say.

My ears heard what my head couldn't think.

My heart felt the emptiness.

Fear floated in my tummy.

My throat was coated in guilt.

My skin oozed with shame.

Anger built in my limbs.

While I looked beyond staring into nothingness.

I continued to see Glenn after he retired. Now I have a long résumé of harp performances, and I discovered I enjoy playing in front of people.

CHAPTER 46: TODAY

One night while drifting off to sleep, I carefully considered sharing my pain and triumphs with an audience. Somewhere in the night, I awoke and realized that most of the pain in my life had been kept hidden—once shared my pain eased. Then I heard a clear, confident voice from within: *What has been the purpose of your life if not to share it with others? In so doing, others may be encouraged by your experiences, thoughts, and feelings.*

Although I have experienced repeated physical, sexual, mental, emotional, and spiritual abuse, both as a child and as an adult, I refuse to be a victim. I was accompanied on my journey by my friends: perseverance, tenacity, and hope. And while I wouldn't want anyone to experience the things I endured, I wouldn't trade my life today.

Each negative experience led to something positive. Being placed in the orphanage took me out of an abusive and neglectful family, and being adopted took me away from the abuses of the orphanage. Marrying Jack took me away from the abuses of my adoptive family and blessed me with Andrew. Meeting Elliot led to the adoption of my children. Time with Steve led me to examine the quality of my life. Concern for myself led me into recovery, and recovery led me to my friends and the harp. And finally, all my experiences led me to telling my story so that others in similar situations might have hope.

Today I continue to have close relationships with Andrew; Ben, who has a son and another on the way; and Lilly. I occasionally visit with Wesley, who has two children. Infrequently I see Sam. Sadly, over the years my brothers Allen and Tom, my sister Kathleen, my stepsisters Mary and Helen, and my dad all passed away. Elliot and Matilda married, and from what I hear they are living happily ever after. At age twenty-three Jan Lee terminated her adoption to me through the courts so she could be adopted by Matilda. My sister Rosie moved to Florida and hasn't returned to Pennsylvania for several years. Connie, Alvin, Ivan, Jeannie, and I get together for reunions. Connie, Ivan, and I live within half an hour of each other and visit more frequently. Connie studied the harp, and we have experienced the joy of performing together. Ivan married for the first time at fifty-seven and has two sons.

Today my life is rich and full. It is balanced between family, good friends, work, play, and creativity. And for what it's worth, I did return to drinking beer on occasion. I live alone, but I am never lonely. Happy, a Lhasa Apso dog who found me one rainy Tuesday night five years ago, lives with me; as does my calico cat, Lovey, whom I adopted last fall. She allows Happy and me to reside with her. The inhabitants of my backyard include turtles, one of which comes to the door if the rain is too heavy.

Creativity frequently tickles me in my heart and soul, and then I know I am called to a new direction. This book has been a calling; I was home at the time and answered it. I have one last letter to write, and I am honored to write it to *you*:

Dear ______________________________ (fill in the blank),

May you take encouragement from my journey—that is the intention. Become *your hero* in your life as I did. Strive to love, respect, and cherish *yourself* as a special gift placed on this earth for a fleeting time. Know that your life has been framed by past experiences when you had no control because you didn't know the meaning of the word.

The difference today is that now *you* are in charge. The past gave you no choices—only the present and future present choice. And only you by your action, or inaction, are in charge today.

Change doesn't come easy—it must be earned, and it's hard, grueling work that sometimes requires twenty-four hours a day (remember, dreams are work). The reward however, is worth it—among all the twisted, snagged, snarly, and entrenched roots, you will find your wings and take flight. You will find your *self*, and that will make all the difference—you will be an agent of change. What a wonderful foundation you will make for future generations!

I offer now some valuable gems from *my* personal healing and give examples that were helpful for me—feel free to add what may work for you. What feels comfortable? What feels like a good place to start? What is not you? What could you try? I don't have all the gems and purposely I left blanks at the end that are personal for you to complete and add on as needed:

Family—select wisely, weed out, don't be duty-bound

Friends—know who it's safe to share what with

Pets—choose well for they become family members

Therapy—like your therapist; if not, drop immediately if not sooner

Work—the most ideal is to like what you do regardless of what it is

Journal writing—doesn't have to be long, but a regular time of day is helpful

Letter writing—give back to the owner what doesn't belong to you (even if the person is dead)

Play—pay attention to your "inner child" who likes to have fun

Hobbies—no matter what: gardening, bowling, reading, flea markets, etc.

Support groups—such as church, addiction groups, mental health

Belief system—organized religion, non-religion, spirituality

Creativity—art, theatre, music, photography, writing, filmmaking, dancing

Relaxation—kick back, breathe deep, meditate, imagine

Grieving—death of a loved one is only one of our losses

Medication—always under the care of a medical doctor

Alternative medicine—chiropractic, herbs, massage, acupuncture, Reiki

Healthy diet—red meat, fowl, fish, fruits, nuts, vegetables, pasta, grains (the key is portion size)

Restful sleep—six to eight hours a night; meditation works wonders

Exercise—whatever you do, like it and work it into your schedule

Spontaneity—go for a walk in the rain, catch a sunset, gaze at the stars

Passion—you will define this; for me it was the harp

Finally, the sage in me counsels: Sometimes life gives you burdens, and sometimes burdens give you life. May your burde[illegible] become your transformed life.

Be well,

Beverly Anne, Julia Mary—Julie

2009